Disinvestment, the Struggle,
and the Future

Disinvestment, the Struggle, and the Future

What Black South Africans Really Think

Mark Orkin

Director of the Community Agency for Social Enquiry
in association with the Institute for Black Research

Ravan Press • Johannesburg

Published by Ravan Press (Pty) Ltd
P O Box 31134, Braamfontein,
Johannesburg, 2017
South Africa

First edition, first impression 1986
First edition, second impression 1986

ISBN 0 86975 305 3

Cover design by Jacqui Bosman

Typeset by Jayset c.c.

Printed by Sigma Press (Pty) Ltd, Pretoria

Contents

Lists of Tables and Figures

Preface

This report, based on a nation-wide survey in September 1985, clearly establishes the fact that a decisive majority of urban black South Africans support some form of disinvestment as a means of helping to end apartheid.

The fact may seem obvious to any sensibly informed observer of the South African scene. But it is fundamentally important. For it corrects the opposite impression created by half a dozen earlier surveys, which claimed to demonstrate that most urban blacks reject disinvestment. This earlier claim, although evidently implausible, was eagerly seized upon by numerous dignitaries — businessmen, politicians and government officials in South Africa, and some statesmen abroad — as the chief moral basis for their defence of foreign investment in South Africa.

Our new survey 'sends a rocket right through their position', as a British diplomat put it. Whatever other justifications might now be advanced by the advocates of investment, they can no longer maintain their posture of deferring to democracy, of seeking to respect the available indications of black opinion.

Conversely, the new survey vindicates both the policies on disinvestment and the consultative procedures of major black trade union federations, political movements, and the South African Council of Churches (SACC). The message reaching the leadership of these organizations was that most blacks in their respective constituencies endorsed economic pressure against apartheid. The organizations took policy accordingly. These policies were dismissed as provocative and elitist by the local functionaries and foreign diplomats.

Our study finds that the policies discerningly reflected the nuances of grass-roots opinion. The charge of elitism can rather be levelled at the dignitaries, in their rush to trust tendentious interpretations of simplistic data over the effective representative processes of the organizations they were condemning.

Some of the respects in which the previous surveys were misconceived and misleading were identified early in the debate by several academics and commentators. But, in matters of social policy and scientific practice alike, criticism is never conclusive and seldom influential. One has to get into the arena and try to do better.

So, in mid-1985 the Community Agency for Social Enquiry (CASE), working in association with the Institute for Black Research (IBR), decided to undertake a new urban sample survey on disinvestment. Our prime aim was to be more adequately sensitive to the black public's actual conception of the issue. In particular, it was evident from the prevailing discussion that disinvestment was not regarded as a simple 'either-or' matter. A distinction was frequently drawn between conditional and total disinvestment, as alternatives to unrestricted investment.

Proceeding on this understanding, we found that a total of *seventy-three per cent of metropolitan blacks actually favour one or the other form of disinvestment*. Nor is this result 'just another point of view'. For our analysis demonstrates where the previous surveys went wrong, and also recovers some of their evidence and incorporates it into a coherent picture of how black attitudes on the issue are hardening over time.

In other words, our investigation offers a new result, provides a more comprehensive conceptual framework, and is thereby able to correct or subsume previous findings. It thus satisfies the three criteria by which a scientific advance is usually said to *refute* its predecessors, rather than merely contradict or qualify them.

There is another respect in which, we believe, the CASE/IBR study constitutes an advance. Instead of just polling disinvestment attitudes, we set them firmly in the context of fundamental social transformation. We located economic pressure along the range of prevalent strategies for dismantling apartheid, from peaceful to violent. We then observed the differing responses to these strategies among the followers of various political tendencies.

According to the figures, the noteworthy black political leaders and organizations are (in descending order of popularity) Nelson Mandela and the ANC, Bishop Desmond Tutu, the UDF, and Chief Mangosuthu Buthelezi and his Inkatha movement. We discovered that only a small proportion of urban blacks nation-wide still support Buthelezi, and that Buthelezi's is the only one of these four tendencies in which there is a majority backing for investment. Among the other three tendencies the feeling is massively in favour of conditional or total disinvestment.

In addition to exploring strategies for change, we considered likely outcomes. Respondents overwhelmingly favoured a unitary over a federal model of the polity, and a socialist over a capitalist vision of the economy.

Revealing similarities and differences between the liberation ideologies of the respective tendencies emerge from these results. When one looks at the overall pattern, one sees that the important axis of conflict in South Africa is not between black and white but between the minority who have thrown in their lot with 'the system' and the mainstream who unequivocally reject it.

The implication is that, for the majority of urban black South Africans, support for disinvestment is not only an important component of their struggle for the future. It is also an acid test of whether or not one actually supports the kind of South Africa they are struggling for. Our study likewise has a dual thrust: to signal to policy-makers in South Africa and abroad the democratic prescriptions with which they will increasingly have to reckon; and, more importantly, to illuminate for the participants in the mainstream the powerful extent to which they are united in their efforts.

Mark Orkin

Johannesburg
April 1986

Acknowledgements

Doing large-scale empirical sociology is like mountain climbing, I would guess, in two important respects.

The first is that the activity is exciting because it is risky. However ingenious one's estimations of the contingencies ahead, the encounter with material reality is likely to be bruising — unless one is lucky. In this bit of sociology we were mostly lucky.

The second similarity is that beneath the excitement is hidden an enormous logistical exercise. For the single person who gets the satisfaction and the publicity of concluding the job, there are supporters halfway up the route, and others out of sight at base-camp, without whom the venture would literally have been impossible.

There are many people on this mountain. John Samuel, one of the co-authors of the idea of CASE several years ago, espoused my vision of the study from the outset and kept us pushing onwards when prospective sponsors backed off. He sets a fine example of how South Africans can retain the initiative in establishing their political possibilities and priorities.

Professor Fatima Meer, Director of the IBR, readily accepted the invitation to associate her Institute with the project. She and Saths Cooper, one of the IBR's trustees, gave generously of their time in shaping the enquiry at the beginning and in reviewing the report at the end. Their ability to link a keen and committed awareness of black macro-political process to the finicky details of survey design helped ensure that the key questions so demonstrably worked.

John Aitcheson was invaluable too, at the beginning and the end and also in the middle: several of the more telling patterns in the analysis derive from his subtle sense of where, in hundreds of pages of tables, it would be profitable to look.

Tom Lodge and Alec Erwin had a signal impact on some of the crucial questions. Beatrice Matlala and Thakane Mbatha re-worked the Zulu and Sotho translations. A couple of major solecisms in my sociological argument were rooted out by Marshall Murphree; the survivors are, as the saying goes, my own achievement.

The South African Council of Churches, its concern with disinvestment made more pressing when its policy decision on the matter aroused a storm of criticism, found the money for the research. The General Secretary, Dr Beyers Naudé, was an exemplary sponsor. In his view, if the results vindicated its policy, the SACC had a foundation of support on which to build; if not, a problem of representativeness to address. Either way, the facts needed to be established and publicized. In the ensuing effort, the perceptive advice of Dr Wolfram Kistner and the warm encouragement of Dan Vaughan were welcome.

Butch Rice, the Research Director of Research Surveys (Pty) Ltd, and Sû Aspinall, his co-ordinator for this project, boldly accepted the challenge of working within irreconcilable constraints of time and cost. Much overtime was also contributed by Audrey Mabasa, Brenda Townsend and her coding team, the punch clerks, and Carol Gidlow. Greg Classen and Errol Nienaber showed a mighty concern for the precision of the computations that was not weakened by thirty-six hours at the terminals without sleep. But the top honours finally go to the interviewers, supervised by Stan Mbatha and Temsi Nkosi. They put their bodies as well as their skills on the line, volunteering to steer piles of questionnaires between comrades and Casspirs during the most violent times that the townships have ever experienced. I was relieved as well as delighted when they found that the respondents were overwhelmingly enthusiastic about the venture. I hope they feel that this report vindicates their determination.

Members of the IBR were inventive in getting the first results into the media. As a next step in disseminating the findings, I undertook a lecture tour of universities abroad. For the considerable labour of setting up addresses, seminars, presentations and subventions at very short notice, I owe thanks to several old and new friends: Tony Marx, Adam Klein, Tom Karis and Benjamin Rivlin, Michael Joseph and Catherine Coles, Dan Aronsohn and Andy Orkin, Walter Allen, Martin Carnoy, John Marcum, Edna Bonacich, Bob Price and Carl Rosberg, Charles Young, Mike Clough, Steven Lukes, and finally Friedl Sellschop and Jackie Cock and Robin Crewe, at − respectively − Princeton, Harvard, SUNY, Dartmouth, McGill, Michigan (Ann Arbor), Stanford, UC (Santa Cruz), UC (Riverside), UC (Berkeley), UC (LA), Monterey, Oxford, and (back home) the University of the Witwatersrand. In many instances student societies made an essential contribution to the organization and the funds. John Marcum co-ordinated California, and genially proved that the phrase need not be an oxymoron. Participants in these occasions will recognise the fruits of their queries and criticisms at many junctures in the following pages.

During the trip I also attended meetings with church groups or voluntary associations in London, Utrecht, Trier and Geneva. These organizations have a depth and endurance to their anti-apartheid activities that is quite inspiring.

This report grew ... and grew ... out of my lecture abroad. Its gestation was nurtured by Pam Thornley, who was a tranquil amanuensis, clippings-clerk, proof-reader, and fellow aficionado of Fowler — a marvellous combination. Johnny van der Riet saw the manuscript through an impressively rapid delivery.

The striking cover was crafted by Jacqui Bosman. Dave Anderson specially adapted the centre-page cartoon, which appeared in a different version in *The Sunday Star*. Ulla Lamos translated my dotty computer graphs into crisp line diagrams.

And then there is Jennifer Glennie, another of the co-authors of the idea of CASE, now my wife and still my friend. She helped sustain my hare-brained determination to undertake the project; somehow met all the demands of her job and our daughter Kate as I hurtled round the country doing the survey and round America and Europe talking about it; made discerning improvements to the questionnaire and write-up; and usefully reminded me that liberation of the political economy includes the home, so that baby-sitting waits for no publisher.

Chapter 1

Introduction: Disinvestment and Democracy in South Africa

Direct investment by foreign companies amounts to about ten per cent of all investment in South Africa, and foreign holdings of South African shares account for another twenty per cent.[1] If the companies concerned were to withdraw or the shares be publicly sold in appreciable proportions, the impact on the South African economy would be massive. A couple of commentators have claimed that Rhodesia after UDI not only survived economic sanctions but ultimately benefited from the experience in having to develop substitutes for imports, and that South Africa would do the same.[2] But even the South African government and its advisors are less confident. They, no less than the business sector and the official opposition in the white parliament,[3] are convinced that foreign investment is indispensable for major capital projects and the creation of new jobs: the Auditor General estimates that such investment accounts for a significant one to one and a half per cent in the economic growth rate in real terms.[4]

Disinvestment thus offers powerful leverage, a means of forcing the South African government to dismantle apartheid. But there is substantial disagreement among experts as well as laymen[5] about the possible disadvantages. How costly will disinvestment be? Will blacks,[6] who presumably can least afford it, have to bear the brunt? If so, are they willing to make the sacrifice?

Consequently, the merit of disinvestment as a strategy for social change has been vigorously debated among anti-apartheid movements during recent months, in South Africa no less than abroad. In the debate, disinvestment is often compared or contrasted with an even more controversial strategy, armed struggle. Indeed, the standpoints of different political movements in South Africa are largely epitomized by the way in which they regard the two strategies, the one peaceful, the other violent.

For example, there is Chief Mangosuthu Gatsha Buthelezi, premier of the KwaZulu homeland authority and leader of Inkatha, the Zulu politico-cultural movement which claims more than a million members. He has been as vociferous as the government in alleging that within South Africa 'disinvestment . . . is championed solely by those who seek to establish a non-capitalist state through the use of violence', and that 'a majority of ordinary black South Africans reject it'.[7]

In sharp contrast is the stance of the African National Congress (ANC), which despite being forced underground by the Nationalist government a quarter of a century ago regularly tops political polls among blacks, aided by the enormous popularity of Nelson Mandela. The ANC insists that foreign companies basically prop up apartheid, so that total disinvestment is as justifiable and necessary in the economic realm as armed struggle is in the military.[8] In April 1986 Winnie Mandela called on the international community to apply 'immediate and total sanctions' against South Africa, as a last non-violent means of toppling apartheid.[9]

In between these positions, some church leaders and organizations — including Desmond Tutu, Archbishop-elect of Cape Town and a recent winner of the Nobel Peace Prize, and the South African Council of Churches (SACC) — affirm that they cannot themselves support violence, even though they can understand how black South Africans feel driven to it.[10] They argue that conditional disinvestment, directed against particular foreign companies that do not comply with specific workplace demands and community responsibilities, is a non-violent strategy powerful enough to be effective against apartheid, yet selective enough not to harm black interests.[11]

Conditional disinvestment is also viewed by most unions as a useful tool against recalcitrant managers of foreign concerns.[12] However, other unions hold out for total disinvestment, alongside political movements like the black-consciousness Azanian People's Organization (AZAPO),[13] and sections of the non-racial United Democratic Front (UDF).[14]

In the absence of free and universal franchise for blacks,[15] and with notable parties such as the ANC and the PAC (Pan African Congress, the Africanist offshoot of the ANC) excluded from the political marketplace, fundamental policy matters such as these cannot be settled by majority vote. In such a context social science acquires the onerous responsibility of discovering how blacks would vote on important questions, if they could. Attitude surveys become surrogates for the democratic process. They are thus quite appropriately taken seriously by policy-makers in government, churches, universities, business, and the media, who for various reasons are sensitive to grass-roots opinion.

This interest in data about black South African attitudes has been especially conspicuous in the disinvestment debate. On the basis of several studies conducted late in 1984 and early in 1985, it was generally believed until very recently that approximately 75% of urban black South Africans opposed disinvestment; or, in other words, that they favoured continued investment over disinvestment by a ratio of 3:1.

These statistics were rapidly accorded great prominence. For instance, they were invoked during 1985 by the US Secretary of State, George Shultz,[16] the US Ambassador to South Africa, Herman Nickel,[17] and the British Assistant Foreign Secretary, Malcolm Rifkind,[18] in defence of their respective governments' reluctance to apply economic sanctions against the South African government.

Similarly, although many prominent white businessmen in South Africa had in 1983 publicly supported the government's introduction of a new constitution which continued the explicit exclusion of blacks from the central political process, they suddenly began to show remarkable solicitude for black opinion when it seemed that this was opposed to disinvestment. For example, in a special edition of *Leadership* magazine dealing with the debate,[19] some twenty thousand copies of which were circulated abroad,[20] several prominent business contributors quoted the 3:1 ratio as part of the argument in favour of continuing investment. Buthelezi cited it too.[21]

Our own recent research shows, however, that this influential figure has been gravely misleading. On an adequately discerning conception of the issue, it emerges that nearly three-quarters of urban black South Africans actually favour some or other form of disinvestment. The new results are not merely different. They also reveal where the earlier studies went wrong. This will be demonstrated in the next chapter of this report. In addition, they set disinvestment in an appropriate context of different political strategies and future options in South Africa and how these are regarded by the major black political groupings. Chapter 3 covers these wider issues. They in turn raise important implications for assessments of viable social change, which are considered in Chapter 4, the conclusion of the report.

Notes

1 Peter Honey, 'Sanctions: South Africa will feel the pinch', *Business Day*, 27 September 1985.

2 'SA stands to gain if US firms pull out', *Business Day*, 5 June 1985; Michael Chester, 'Euphoria of SA is cracked at last', *The Sunday Star*, 11 August 1985; Martin Spring, 'Those disinvestment threats against us could yet boomerang', *The Star*, 29 August 1985.

3 Michael Chester, 'Foreign cash vital as 200 000 jobs axed', *The Star*, 7 January 1986; Phillip van Niekerk, 'Trade boycotts more damaging', *Rand Daily Mail*, 22 March 1985; 'Disinvestment: warning going overseas on big job loss', *The Citizen*, 30 March 1985.

4 'Investment holds key', *Business Day*, 16 April 1985; Michael Chester, 'Urbanisation now key to economic growth', *The Star*, 11 September 1985. See also 'Battle looming in SA over disinvestment, warns Nickel', *The Star*, 8 February 1985.

5 Contrast A. Spandau, *Economic Boycott Against South Africa* (Cape Town: Juta, 1979) and Lawrence Schlemmer, 'The dynamic of sanctions', *Leadership* (June 1985), 39-43, with Stephen Gelb, 'Unemployment and the disinvestment debate', *SA Labour Bulletin*, 10:6 (May 1985), 54-66, and M.O. Sutcliffe and P.A. Wellings, 'Disinvestment and black worker "attitudes" in South Africa: a critical comment', forthcoming in *Review of African Political Economy*.

6 We shall be using the term 'black' in the restrictive sense, to refer only to people classified by the government as Africans, because our sample did not include 'Coloureds' and Indians.

7 Mangosuthu G. Buthelezi, 'Inkatha says no', *Leadership* (June 1985), 66-68 (p.68). See also Chief Mangosuthu G. Buthlezi, 'It's now the democratic process versus violence', *The Star*, 30 January 1986.

8 Phillip van Niekerk, 'Racial dilemma of disinvestment', *Rand Daily Mail*, 22 March 1985; M. Hough, 'The ANC after Nkomati: negotiate or escalate?', *The South Africa Foundation News*, August 1985; 'Tambo in his own words', *Weekly Mail*, 10-16 January 1986.

9 'Winnie's gag goes at last', *The Sunday Star*, 6 April 1986. The statement was her first in a decade to be quoted by the press in South Africa, after her banning order was found to be legally invalid.

10 Estelle Trengove, 'Passive resistance: people losing faith – Naudé', *The Star*, 18 September 1985; Carol Lazar, 'A day in the life of Tutu', *The Sunday Star*, 10 November 1985.

11 Carol Lazar, 'A day in the life of Tutu', *op. cit.*; Beyers Naudé, 'Statements to the delegation of the EEC regarding the current crisis in South Africa', mimeo, 30 August 1985.

12 'FOSATU international policy statement, April 1984' and 'CUSA statement on the Kennedy visit', *SA Labour Bulletin*, 10:6 (May 1985), 44-46.

13 'UDF takes stand on disinvestment', *The Star*, 13 June 1985.

14 *Ibid.* See also Phillip van Niekerk, 'Racial dilemma of disinvestment', *op. cit.*

15 Blacks have a right to vote in elections for the homelands legislative authority corresponding to their particular ethnic group. This is what the government means when it says blacks enjoy universal franchise. But few blacks outside the homelands recognize the standing of these authorities, not least because elected members of opposition parties are in most cases outnumbered by nominated chiefs and headmen. So the percentage polls are abysmally low, as noted, for example, in the *Survey of Race Relations in South Africa 1983* (Johannesburg: SA Institute of Race Relations, 1984), p.350; and there is no doubt that this arrangement is not what urban blacks mean when they demand 'the vote'.

16 'Address by Secretary of State George Shultz on United States-South African relations', National Press Club, Washington, D.C., 16 April 1985.

17 Herman Nickel, 'American realities', *Leadership* (June 1985), 22-26 (p.26).

18 John Battersby, 'Britain's Rifkind says: "Sanctions do not work"', *Rand Daily Mail*, 14 December 1984; 'Rifkind says blacks divided on sanctions', *The Star*, 24 April 1985.

19 *Leadership* (June 1985). For example, Tony Bloom, 'The great paradox', 60-65 (p.65); John H. Chettle, 'A Capitol offence', 72-76 (p.72).

20 Michael Chester, 'Harry O warns sanctions lobby', *The Star*, 6 June 1985.

21 Neil Lurssen, 'Kennedy arrogant, says Buthelezi', *The Star*, 4 February 1985.

Chapter 2

White Fancies and Black Facts about Disinvestment

To disinvest or not: is that the question?

The important initial studies on black attitudes to disinvestment were conducted by Professor Lawrence Schlemmer of the Centre for Applied Social Science at the University of Natal in Durban. He administered two surveys during 1984: the first among 551 male production workers in three major industrial centres, and the second among a general sample of 1 000 blacks from all major metropolitan areas, covering women, young people, pensioners and unemployed as well as workers. In both instances Schlemmer found that his respondents apparently favoured investment over disinvestment by a ratio of approximately 3:1.[1]

The key feature to note is that this ratio derives from dichotomous questions. In other words, the matter was posed in an 'either-or' fashion: Is disinvestment a good thing or a bad thing? Should overseas people and banks and companies stop or continue their economic involvement?[2]

This dichotomous approach was then replicated three times, at the taxpayers' expense, by the government's Human Sciences Research Council (HSRC),[3] on large samples drawn from the Pretoria-Witwatersrand-Vaal (PWV) region surrounding Johannesburg. The point of concentrating on the PWV is that half the country's urban blacks live in the region, and approximately two-thirds of industrial production is concentrated there. The HSRC found that the 3:1 ratio in favour of investment was sustained between June 1984 and May 1985, except for a slight dip during Senator Edward Kennedy's tour of South Africa.

So the whole issue seemed cut and dried. But late in August 1985 the London *Sunday Times* published the results of a survey it had commissioned from the South African subsidiary of the Gallup polling organization.[4] In one question respondents were asked whether 'other countries are right or wrong to impose economic sanctions unless South Africa agrees to get rid of the apartheid system'. Slightly more than three-quarters thought they were right, thereby apparently reversing the central finding of the earlier studies.

At this stage confusion reigned. Either black opinion was hopelessly volatile, or else social science was hopelessly inaccurate at measuring it. In any
case, policy-makers had an excuse to ignore it.

However, at that time our interviewers were in the field, and we were
soon able to extract our results. These resolved the inconsistency.

The salience of conditional disinvestment: the CASE/IBR result

The new study was conceived by the author of this report, and conducted
under the auspices of the Community Agency for Social Enquiry (CASE),
in association with the Institute for Black Research (IBR) of the University
of Natal. Research Surveys (Pty) Ltd of Cape Town handled the field-work
and computation.

The CASE/IBR sample covered 800 black respondents over sixteen years
of age, including workers, unemployed, women, students, and pensioners. Respondents were randomly selected in appropriate proportions from
all ten major metropolitan areas of South Africa.

These areas fall into four regions. The PWV region comprises Pretoria,
Johannesburg and Soweto, the Reef and the Vaal triangle; the Natal region,
Durban and Pietermaritzburg; and the Cape region, Port Elizabeth, East
London, and Cape Town. Respondents from the tenth area, Bloemfontein,
were too few to be analysed separately, and were included with the PWV.
The sample size ensures that the probable percentage margin of error on
any particular response is at most 4%, and usually better than 3%.

Details of the sample breakdown, remarks on the interviewing, and other
technical considerations are covered in the methodological note in the Appendix. But it is worth emphasizing here that most prospective interviewees
who came up in the sample were willing to be approached, and evidently
regarded the interviews as a valuable opportunity for their opinions to be
heard and taken seriously.

Similarly, refusals by respondents to answer questions (analysed in the
methodological note in the Appendix) were fairly evenly distributed, suggesting that respondents were not appreciably inhibited by the repressive
social context.

The central tenet of our study was that disinvestment has to be conceived
as a three-way rather than a two-way issue, to be true to the actual distribution of black public opinion. In other words, a trichotomous choice has to
be posed instead of the dichotomies used in the previous studies. This intu-
ition derived from our reading of the way the debate was being waged in
the black press and in politically informed circles.

The notion of an intermediate position, between unrestricted investment and total disinvestment, has been current ever since 1975. In that year Rev. Leon Sullivan proposed that American companies operating in South Africa should agree to abide by a set of employment principles. The Sullivan principles were given renewed import when the obligations of signatories were made more stringent at the end of 1984.[5] Early in 1985 Bishop Desmond Tutu returned from his Nobel Prize trip, having developed and publicly espoused a position of conditional disinvestment during his many meetings with statesmen overseas.[6] At the same time the two major black trade union federations, CUSA and FOSATU, were beginning to receive publicity for their policies, adopted in 1984, in favour of conditional disinvestment. These policies involved even stronger conditions on investment than those of Sullivan or Tutu, notably the recognition of trade unions by the foreign companies under scrutiny.[7] And at mid-year the SACC adopted a resolution at the annual meeting of its council, supporting conditional disinvestment.[8]

So by the time the CASE/IBR study was conceived, the option of conditional disinvestment, falling between free investment and total disinvestment, was being widely canvassed. We were accordingly careful to present our respondents with the three possibilities. The full question and the basic results are set out in Table 1.

As the table shows, the total disinvestment option was selected by approximately one-quarter of the sample (24%). But it did not follow that the balance assented to unrestricted investment: in fact, only a further quarter of the sample (26%) did so. The remaining half (49%) opted for conditional disinvestment, agreeing that 'foreign firms should not be allowed to invest here unless they actively pressure the government to end apartheid, and recognize the trade unions chosen by the workers'.[9]

Respondents did not feel that the issue was fanciful. In a supplementary item (Question 6 in the Appendix), they were asked whether they believed that disinvestment would actually have the effect of bringing the government under pressure to end apartheid. Only a third were doubtful. Logically enough, they tended to be those who had favoured free investment; plus, one might guess, some cynics from the disinvestment camps.

It will be seen from Table 1 that we defined the respective positions in our main disinvestment question so that respondents could be sure of what we were referring to, and we could be sure of what question they thought they were answering. We also gave the most typical motivation for each position, and an indication of the tendencies which supported it. This approach was central to the enquiry. We are convinced that the customary style of attitude polls, which is to present abstract issues for consideration

Table 1   The CASE/IBR question on disinvestment

A lot of foreign companies and banks, that is companies and banks from overseas, do business in South Africa. They lend money to the government or businessmen, or they run factories here. This is called foreign investment. People and groups in South Africa and overseas have different ideas about foreign investment. There are three main views. Which of the three views do you support most?

Per cent

— The first view encourages investment. This view says that foreign firms help South Africa to grow, so they should be encouraged to invest here freely. This view is supported by PW Botha and the Nationalist Government, by businessmen like Harry Oppenheimer, by Chief Mangosuthu Gatsha Buthelezi and Inkatha, and other homeland leaders.   26

— The second view wants to limit or restrict investment. This view says that foreign firms should not be allowed to invest here unless they actively pressure the government to end apartheid, and recognize the trade unions chosen by the workers. This view is supported by Bishop Tutu, by the trade unions in FOSATU and CUSA, and by the SA Council of Churches.   49

— The third view wants no investment. This view says that foreign firms only help to keep apartheid alive and exploit blacks, so foreign firms should not be allowed to remain here at all. This view is supported by the ANC and the PAC, AZAPO, many members of the UDF, and some trade unions.   24

— Don't know.   1
                                             100
                                        (n = 800)

in isolation, effectively constitutes respondents as self-seeking and private individuals, and thereby tends to bias their answers towards the economistic, market-oriented answers which suit business or the capitalist state. For better or worse, when citizens in a democracy go to the vote, issues are conceived in a context of parties and personalities. We wanted our survey to approximate to democratic political choice. So we sought to provide the context, using the vocabulary and examples by which the views were typically being characterized in everyday discussion.

It follows that respondents might have been 'cued' by the political context we supplied, in cases where they were unsure of their feelings on the issue. But because this mix of motivations is very much what would have applied had disinvestment been an issue in an election, our approach, far from biassing the answers, gives them more realism and predictive substance. In any event, respondents were given the opportunity in a prior question to indicate which tendency they preferred, independently of the disinvestment issue. As we shall see below, high proportions of them 'cross-voted', i.e., they did not choose the disinvestment option corresponding to their preferred political tendency. Moreover, cross-voting occurred to differing extents in different tendencies, suggesting that respondents did not feel bullied by the context we supplied.

In this respect, our approach to expressing the question largely followed that recommended by Schlemmer. He has previously argued that the good social surveyor will compensate for the lack of 'background effects and supporting evidence for or against the issues at hand' available in a real-life situation by 'providing fairly lengthy explanations on the issues canvassed and by stating fairly complex political choices in very simple and graphic language'.[10] He also remarks, as we do above, that an important respect in which surveys do not adequately approximate to referenda is that respondents to a questionnaire will not have received 'particular guidance to the expression of opinion' from political leaders. Where our approach then differed is that Schlemmer bowed to the shortcoming even though he explicitly recognized the consequence that 'among both black and white respondents, the expression of political attitudes in [the Buthelezi Report] is likely to err slightly or moderately on the side of caution and conservatism'.[11] We sought instead to avoid the shortcoming, by attempting to provide, in addition to the explanations and background information Schlemmer recommends, indicative political orientations for each of the possible policy options.

It was especially important that we did so on the disinvestment issue, because the information and guidance available to black survey respondents was not so much incomplete as selective and tendentious: partly because many of the proponents of one or other form of disinvestment were in detention or exile and could not be quoted, and partly because of the heavily pro-investment editorial line of the white-oriented newspapers and the South African Broadcasting Corporation (SABC).

As one observer of the media remarked, 'Newspapers and journals have so far published hundreds of thousands of words on [the subject of disinvestment], and the SABC has devoted considerable broadcasting time to spokesmen of many shades, in order, it appears, to persuade us of one thing: "Disinvestment is bad". Prominent in these programmes was the predictable queue of homeland leaders and other black spokesmen whose opposition to disinvestment is well known. What has been generally missing, particularly in the case of the SABC's programmes, has been the voices of those who *favour* disinvestment.'[12]

It becomes clear that, had we omitted the spectrum of leadership indications from the explanatory context which we provided for the main

questions, at a methodological level we would have been introducing a conceptual bias by abstracting from the actual nature of political process we
were seeking to model; at an empirical level we would have been know-
ingly countenancing a substantial bias in the balance of influences bearing
on the responses we were soliciting; and at a policy level we would have
been colluding with the media in the perpetuation of the dominant ideolo-
gy. We thus believe that our alternative was technically, practically and
ethically preferable.

How attitudes have hardened over time
The new result obtained by CASE and the IBR makes sense in several
respects. The first is that it explains the apparent contradictions among the
various earlier studies.

Schlemmer and the HSRC had in effect found that approximately three-
quarters of their respondents would oppose total disinvestment, when confronted with a dichotomy. This is depicted by the shaded area in Figure
1a. Using a different question, the London *Sunday Times* had in effect found
that approximately three-quarters of their respondents would oppose free
investment when confronted with a dichotomy, as shown by the shaded area
in Figure 1b.

The confusion arose because the respective sets of respondents were being presented with 'either-or' questions that conceptually overlapped. In
both instances, the dichotomies were failing to distinguish those people,
situated between the quarter of respondents at each extreme, who actually
favoured the intermediate position. This may be clearly seen if one superim-
poses the two diagrams, as has been done in Figure 1c. The cross-shaded
portion in the middle suggests that, had someone clearly differentiated the
option, half of urban black South Africans would have favoured conditional disinvestment ... which is exactly what we did, and what we found!

In fact it is partly coincidental that our percentages reconcile so neatly
with the composite we have constructed from the previous studies. After
all, the various questions were worded somewhat differently. More importantly, about a year had elapsed between Schlemmer's surveys and ours.
One would expect some change in the distribution of opinion over that
period, especially with disinvestment beginning to be extensively covered
in the media and discussed by the public.

When one finds a suitable bench-mark for comparison over time, it turns
out that our finding reflects changes which it would be plausible to expect.
Interestingly, the bench-mark is to be found in the Schlemmer surveys. In
the full technical report of his first survey amongst the 551 workers is an

Fig. 1 The salience of conditional disinvestment

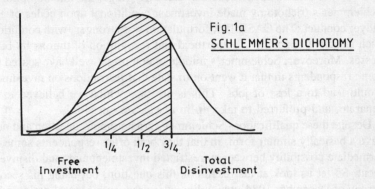

Fig. 1a
SCHLEMMER'S DICHOTOMY

1/4   1/2   3/4

Free
Investment

Total
Disinvestment

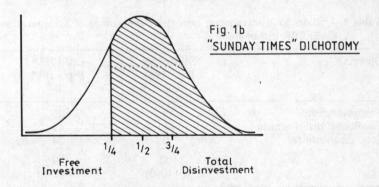

Fig. 1b
"SUNDAY TIMES" DICHOTOMY

1/4   1/2   3/4

Free
Investment

Total
Disinvestment

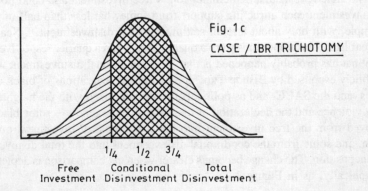

Fig. 1c
CASE / IBR TRICHOTOMY

1/4   1/2   3/4

Free
Investment

Conditional
Disinvestment

Total
Disinvestment

account of a three-way question on disinvestment, with which we can draw a suggestive comparison.[13]

Given the content of the debate at that early stage, the middle option in Schlemmer's trichotomy made investment conditional upon codes of employer conduct. The CASE/IBR formulation was stronger, with conditions such as active opposition to apartheid and recognition of unions by businesses. Moreover, Schlemmer's middle option might well have scared off some respondents in that it went on to state that restrictions on investment would lead to a loss of jobs. This is an issue which we believed to be separate, and preferred to take up in a separate question.

Despite these qualifications Schlemmer's trichotomous question and ours have a basically similar form, in that they both offer respondents some intermediate possibility between unrestricted investment and total disinvestment. So let us look at his results on this question, but using his second survey of December 1984, which like ours drew on a general nation-wide metropolitan sample. The comparison is displayed in Table 2.

Table 2 Attitudes to disinvestment, over time: comparison of Schlemmer and CASE/IBR trichotomies

Option	Schlemmer Dec. 1984 %	CASE/IBR Sept. 1985 %
Free investment	47	26
Conditional disinvestment	44	49
Total disinvestment	9	24
	100	99
	(n = 1000)	(n = 796)

The table reveals that Schlemmer found free investment and conditional disinvestment each attracting support from somewhat less than half of his sample, with only about a tenth settling for total disinvestment.[14] Nearly a year later, our proportions were a quarter, a half and a quarter respectively.

What has probably happened is that — as conditional disinvestment was publicly espoused by Bishop Tutu, the two major federations of black unions, and the SACC, and as political attitudes polarized with the heightening violence and the declaration of the State of Emergency — some blacks moved from the free investment into the conditional disinvestment position, and some from the conditional disinvestment into the total disinvestment position. The change becomes clearer when the comparison is depicted graphically, as in Figure 2.

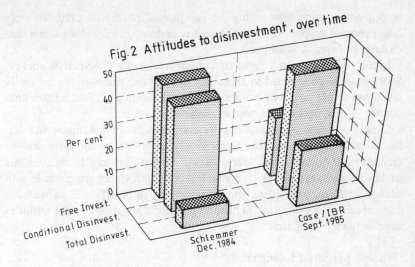

Fig. 2 Attitudes to disinvestment, over time

Look at the left-hand set of pillars in the figure, reflecting the percentages which Schlemmer found. Imagine a transfer from the rear pillar to the middle; and another transfer from the middle pillar to the front. Schlemmer's findings are thereby transformed into the CASE/IBR findings of a year later, shown as the right-hand set of pillars.

In sum, there has been an aggregate shift in attitude towards the radical end of the spectrum. Evidently, black public opinion on disinvestment has not been volatile or contradictory, but has undergone a gradual and quite intelligible shift as the circumstances have evolved. This shift can, moreover, be quite coherently displayed by available sociological methods, provided one uses adequately discerning questions to tap the distinctions which the public are actually drawing.

The issue that does arise is how Schlemmer's more discriminating three-way result was repeatedly passed over in favour of the simplistic, dichotomous version that engendered so much confusion; especially when he found that the conditional disinvestment option, even before it had begun to receive much coverage, was proving nearly as popular as free investment. Part of the problem may have been that secretaries of state, or the coiners of newspaper headlines, can only juggle two numbers in their heads at a time. But part of the problem was this: when Schlemmer himself referred to the three-way question in the initial popular summaries[15] of his findings (the summaries which were presumably used by the policy-makers and the press), he did not mention how highly the conditional position scored. He only remarked that support for total disinvestment dropped very low when a conditional position was allowed.

More recently, in a couple of comments on the CASE/IBR survey, Schlemmer has attempted to argue that his and our findings are not really discrepant.[16] He contends that the studies were similar in finding that one-quarter of respondents supported total disinvestment.

This is misleading, since it illicitly compares his dichotomous distribution to our trichotomous one. Surprisingly, although he concedes that his dichotomous question was 'very stark',[17] he prefers not to mention his trichotomous question, which is much more comfortably comparable with ours in its form, and indeed allows one neatly to illustrate — as we have done above — a point that Schlemmer himself advances,[18] that attitudes have hardened over time.

'We are prepared to suffer'

There are two other important aspects of the heated argument about disinvestment. What is the possible impact of disinvestment on unemployment? And are blacks willing to endure the hardships that may be involved? The former question involves economic realities. We shall briefly attempt to disentangle them in the next section. The latter is a sociological question, regarding people's everyday perceptions and priorities. Let us turn to it now.

The claims of black leaders in this regard are quite contradictory. Buthelezi is in no doubt, from mass meetings he has held, that blacks endorse his rejection of disinvestment because the policy will increase their 'poverty and misery' and entail 'the destruction of the South African economy'. In this, he claims, 'the majority of ordinary black South Africans find common cause with a wide range of white allies'.[19]

The opposing assertion, as made for example by Bishop Tutu, is that 'Blacks have said quite clearly: "We are prepared to stand that suffering"'.[20] Their reasoning has been vividly summarized by a black journalist: 'The suffering unleashed by sanctions — despite what paid puppets of the system have to say — will be worth the pain because, unlike in the past three hundred years when blacks suffered pointlessly under various white governments, at the end a society ordered with the will and consent of all the people will emerge.'[21]

At stake is a trade-off in people's minds between public political commitments and private economic costs. We explored it by asking respondents whether they would wish to back off or stand by their declared positions on disinvestment if they knew that relatively few, or indeed that many, blacks would suffer unemployment as a consequence. The results were then combined into an index (see Question 7 in the Appendix). A quarter (26%) of the respondents are 'hard-line', much as in the disinvestment question, and would advocate their position whatever the cost. A further quarter (25%) would sustain their stance if few, but not many, jobs were to be lost. The remaining half of the sample (48%) would be cautious if sacrifice had to be involved.

This outcome highlights another respect in which the CASE/IBR trichotomous approach to surveying disinvestment was intuitively plausible. An ordinary black person in the street is likely to be implacably hostile to apartheid; keen to hasten its demise; yet — as a wage-earner with several dependants, or as one of those dependants — anxiously aware of the daily grind of survival, at a time of enduring recession and rising unemployment. It seems likely that many such respondents are looking to conditional disinvestment for a strategy which could help to end apartheid while threatening their everyday livelihood as little as possible.

It would seem to follow that respondents who were employed might have different priorities on this issue of jobs from respondents who were unemployed. There is a marginal difference (53% of the unemployed compared to 46% of the employed fall into the 'cautious' category of the index), but not enough to be statistically significant. Evidently the prospective benefits of overthrowing apartheid are equally appealing (although perhaps in different ways) to those with and without a job. A significant difference does show up on the disinvestment question, but it is slight: the unemployed are more likely than the employed to favour free investment, by 31% to 25%. It is clear, then, that the unemployed are not destructive desperadoes but people whose considerable political concerns are tempered, mildly, by their personal straits.

To summarize, even those who are already suffering are in the main prepared to endure more, provided it is within reason and will help unseat white oppression. The cartoon by Andy which is reproduced overleaf pointedly illustrates the sentiment.

In the foregoing analysis it was illuminating to examine the pattern of statistically significant differences among responses across both the disinvestment and the unemployment questions simultaneously, because there is of course a very strong association between the two variables. Further examination of the data in this manner reveals two consistent profiles, which one might interpret as characterizing 'active' versus 'acquiescent' citizens. The radical responses tend to be above average amongst 'active' citizens: those who belong to a political party, club or trade union, and who are better educated. Conversely, support for free investment, and reluctance to

see blacks lose jobs because of disinvestment, tend to be higher amongst 'acquiescent' citizens: those who say they never read newspapers, and belong to no voluntary associations. Xhosa speakers have above average representation in the 'active' category and Zulu speakers in the 'acquiescent', coinciding with the fact that Xhosa speakers have more formal education on average than Zulu speakers.

However, these contrasts most certainly do not imply that supporters of disinvestment are restricted, as Schlemmer contends, to 'a socio-economic and political elite, much less dependent on the industrial system for their material security and status'.[22] In fact there is no statistically distinguishable difference between those earning less than R500 per month and those earning more, in the extent of their opposition to free investment; nor among students, white-collar employees, and blue-collar workers. (In fact, the only difference among these categories in regard to disinvestment is that white-collar employees are slightly more likely than students or workers to support conditional rather than total disinvestment.) In sum, supporters of one or other form of disinvestment do tend to be more educated, informed and involved, as we noted in the previous paragraph. In other words, they are more politically aware. It would be a rather patronizing mistake to infer that they are therefore well-heeled.

A couple of other features are informative: religion and age. Firstly, members of the black independent churches are rather more inclined than members of other religious groupings to oppose disinvestment, and also to worry about its employment implications. Perhaps that is why the head of the largest of these churches, the Zion Christian Church, is the one black cleric whom PW Botha voluntarily consults. Even so, more than two-thirds of black independent members supported one or other form of disinvestment, and both the Apostolic Faith Mission and an association of independent churches have issued statements voicing strong opposition to the government and distancing themselves from the 'widely held view' that they are 'pro-apartheid'.[23]

Secondly, as one might have guessed, greater support for total rather than conditional disinvestment was evident among the youngest category of respondents. It might be thought that this was because unemployment is not yet a real worry for this group. However, the various age categories are effectively indistinguishable in their readiness to risk unemployment. Youngsters are evidently no less aware of, and responsible about, economic exigencies than their elders, but — being more radical — are perhaps less readily persuaded that total disinvestment will actually be more to their economic disadvantage than conditional disinvestment.

These finer relationships have an additional interest. By showing that the data move as one would expect in respects which one does know about, one is inclined to trust the material when new relationships emerge which one would not have known to expect.

Key issues: divestment/disinvestment, robots/jobs, codes/unions
Having fleshed out the basic results on disinvestment and their possible consequences for employment, we can now take up the important considerations which the results pose for disinvestment policy. Two related distinctions are helpful. Although they are too technical to have been canvassed as issues in the survey, they allow us to consider in some detail how categories of respondents might react to the possible policies. The first distinction — to use American terminology for the moment — is between *divestment* and *disinvestment*. Divestment occurs when a church or university or city authority, for example, sells shares in a foreign company because that company does business in South Africa, or does it in an unacceptable fashion. By contrast, disinvestment occurs when the foreign company closes or sells its South African operation and withdraws, repatriating what assets it can.

The British rendition of this distinction is confusingly different. What the Americans call divestment, i.e., when the owner of shares sells them, the British refer to as disinvestment. And what the Americans call disinvestment, i.e., when the company pulls out, the British refer to as disengagement. We shall follow the American usage.

In the case of divestment, then, the shares sold by one owner are simply bought by another. But the sale is not pointless. Undertaken publicly and as part of a specific campaign, it is intended to bring the company concerned under the pressure of public scrutiny, so that its head office will require the management of the South African subsidiary to behave better. This process undoubtedly occurs. The investor relations manager of a prominent American computer firm complained that queries concerning its South African operations used to occupy a day per month, but by late 1985 occupied a week.[24] An executive of another US company observed that 'although we get ten per cent of our profits in South Africa, it's taking up fifty per cent of our boardroom time'.[25]

It is thus apparent that *divestment* pressure quite probably improves black employees' conditions and opportunities in South Africa,[26] and, of itself, does not necessarily cause South Africans to lose jobs. However, the company may in due course feel that its profit is not worth the extra effort, and decide to *disinvest*, i.e., withdraw. In this event, it is not impossible that its operation is entirely taken over as a going concern by other foreign or South African investors. But in many instances the operation will be scaled down or closed altogether, resulting in retrenchments and the destruction of processes that create employment and wealth — as occurred with the closure at the end of 1985 of the Alfa Romeo car plant near Brits, which put several hundred workers on the streets.

Accordingly, some trade unionists have lately been favouring divestment while opposing disinvestment.[27] In support of the former, they argue that if management is subjected to foreign shareholder pressure, it will be more responsive to South African workers' interests. But in general they oppose the latter, regarding the repatriation of the proceeds of disinvestment as the theft of assets which have been created to a considerable extent by local black workers and which should be retained within the country to be turned to their advantage under a different, future political dispensation.

This use of the distinction would presumably appeal to those respondents who in principle support disinvestment as a means of applying economic pressure on the government but are anxious about its possible effect on employment.

A second distinction becomes relevant here, concerning the extent to which foreign investment evidently generates employment or not.[28] Some investment clearly does create jobs, such as a loan to build a labour-intensive plant. Some clearly does not, such as when the South African government borrows from Peter to repay Paul — for example, from a foreign commercial bank to pay an IMF loan which is falling due. However, most cases lie between these neat extremes, and need to be carefully considered. Even investing in plant can be a mixed blessing. General Motors, based in the Eastern Cape where unemployment is running at fifty per cent, installed a robot on one of its motor production lines. Although management pointed out that this innovation did not destroy any jobs, some 465 workers were being temporarily laid off at that very time because of the recession in the industry, and 320 workers had been retrenched elsewhere in the factory a short while before that.[29]

The point can be made more generally. Much foreign investment, especially that of large trans-national corporations, uses capital-intensive techniques, so that jobs have not been created that would have been, had the production been undertaken by smaller local concerns. Moreover, the presence of the trans-nationals then obliges other local concerns to be similarly capital-intensive in order to compete.[30]

This feature of foreign investment becomes evident when, using United States companies as an initial illustration, one categorizes by race the 170 000 workers in directly-owned, US-controlled employment.[31] The ratio of white to black (i.e., African) employees is approximately 1:1, compared to a South African average of approximately 1:3 in manufacturing and 1:9 in mining.[32] The pattern in other foreign companies is similar. The overall ratio of whites to blacks among the 600 000 South Africans in foreign employ turns out to be 1:2. In other words, foreign companies tend to have a much higher proportion of whites than local companies. This reflects the overwhelmingly skill-based nature of their operations, whether in the manufacturing or service sectors.

These figures have a startling implication, which has been hitherto little known. Recall that unemployment, nationally, is presently running at about 5% for whites, compared to 25% for blacks. Now suppose that all directly-owned American companies were to withdraw overnight. When categorized by race, their employees comprise more than 3% of the total white work force, but less than 1% of the black.[33] So white unemployment would rise from 5% to 8%, i.e., an *increase* of some 60%; whereas black unemployment would rise from 25% to 26%, an *increase* of only 4%.

Obviously, our supposition has been very crude: in some cases blacks might be laid off more readily than whites; in others, a local company taking over might have a more labour-intensive approach; and there would be ripple effects. However, it establishes the point that white South Africans would experience the impact of disinvestment more heavily than blacks, as regards the respective percentage increases in prevailing unemployment. One may now understand why white businessmen are 'jumping around like scalded cats',[34] as Sheena Duncan, then President of the Black Sash, put it. The contrast also suggests that Chief Buthelezi is wrong in claiming that blacks would be the first to suffer from disinvestment. Rather, it tends to substantiate the view we noted at the beginning of the previous section, that the unemployment consequences of disinvestment pressures are a price that blacks — having suffered so much already for so long — would be quite prepared to pay,[35] in that disinvestment would impinge on them much less than on whites in the comparative sense we have identified.

Facts such as these encourage the UDF, AZAPO, the ANC, the PAC and some unions in their advocacy of total rather than conditional economic sanctions, and in pressing for actual disinvestment rather than mere divestment (or, as the British would phrase it, in pressing for actual disengagement rather than mere disinvestment).

These parties would also point to other factors. At best, foreign companies are fair-weather friends, interested in South Africa only so long as they can do well enough to offset the nuisance value of being there. This actually became evident before the current disinvestment campaign took hold. Beginning with the Soweto revolt in 1976,[36] and to an increasing extent after the next phase of unrest in 1980, the balance of foreign investment has moved overwhelmingly away from long-term involvement in production towards short-term bank loans. For example, as rates of return to American companies dropped from the 20% they had enjoyed in 1980 to 5% in 1984,[37] US direct investment dropped from a high of $2.6bn in 1981 to $1.8bn by the end of 1984 and to $1.3bn by early 1986,[38] while US bank loans increased 450%[39] between 1981 and early 1985, to a total of $4.2bn.[40]

At worst, foreign companies behave like what Max Weber called 'bounty capitalists', involved in South Africa precisely because they can achieve huge profits in primary production using legally enforced migrant labour, or realize high selling prices for manufactured products in the relatively uncompetitive market, or exact generous payments for patents and know-how.[41]

Moreover, their actual record as employers is dismal. For instance, although the Sullivan code has been on the scene since 1975, on a recent count only some 135 of some 300 American companies doing business in South Africa had signed it, half of them having only signed in the previous year as disinvestment pressure mounted.[42] It might be thought that the signatories would include most of the high-profile concerns with large workforces: in fact, less than half of blacks employed in American companies are covered by the code.[43] Nor are those who declare their adherence to the Sullivan code or its EEC counterpart necessarily exemplary. A recent review found that, of some 350 foreign companies that actually were signatories of some or other employment code, only a quarter were recognizing the trade unions of the workers' choice.[44] And a 1984 survey of 107 British companies showed that seven paid 'starvation wages' to blacks, while a further 39 paid less than the EEC minimum.[45]

All in all — so the total disinvestment argument goes — capitalism is intrinsically exploitative, and foreign capital is its most unacceptable face.

The protagonists of more selective action might reply that some degree of private enterprise is necessary, at least for the while; that foreign companies, although intrinsically no more ethical than local ones, are more vulnerable to pressure from abroad; and that an increase in black unemployment because of disinvestment, although it might be marginal in percentage terms, would still betoken numerous empty bellies. They accordingly recommend that international corporate head offices continue to be pressed by the threat of *divestment* to secure adequate behaviour from their South African subsidiaries, on the understanding that those which prove to be obdurate should then be forced by their governments to *disinvest*.[46]

As importantly, with regard to criteria for satisfactory conduct, the advocates of conditional disinvestment have become increasingly dismissive of employment codes, pointing out that the codes were devised by foreign management rather than local workers, are not mandatory or enforceable, are poorly monitored, and therefore have failed to bring about any significant changes.[47] They demand instead that corporations actively press for an end to apartheid; recognize unions, whereby workers are empowered to identify and resolve relevant issues for themselves; and be penalized by the metropolitan governments for breaches of internationally accepted labour standards.[48]

Survey data should not be expected to resolve such particular policy considerations. But they can inform the debate. So it is worth noting that we canvassed black opinion on the more stringent demand, for disinvestment (companies being forced by their governments to pull out of South Africa), rather than merely divestment (companies being pressed to change by shareholders' threats to sell their shares). Even so, three-quarters of the respondents demanded some degree of economic sanction, and half were prepared to have blacks bear a more considerable cost than, as we have shown, would in fact be involved.

Economic sanctions versus political expedients

Compared to the black expectations of foreign economic pressure discussed above, the sanctions package reluctantly announced by President Reagan in September 1985 amounts to a playful tap on the corporate wrist.

The previous year had seen massive protests on campuses and outside South African diplomatic offices across the United States. In that time, ten states, thirty major city authorities, and fifty-five universities — including Yale, Columbia, Rutgers and Dartmouth — had publicly declared that they were totally divesting themselves of shares in companies with South African subsidiaries, or else making their investments conditional on the subsidiaries' being highly rated under the Sullivan principles.[49]

This pressure obviously hurt: in the same period, some eighteen American multinationals, among them several top companies such as PanAm, Singer, Helena Rubenstein, Pepsi Cola, and Apple Computers announced that they were reducing their involvement in South Africa or leaving altogether, although only Apple asserted that it was acting for moral rather than commercial reasons.[50] Phibro-Salomon, the huge American trading conglomerate, decided to withdraw entirely despite the fact that its single largest shareholder is said to be Harry Oppenheimer, who opposes disinvestment.[51] And ten prominent companies that had declared their determination to stay, including General Motors, Burroughs, Mobil, IBM and Caltex, set up a corporate council to help local business lobby for reform.[52]

In tune with these developments, a joint conference of the House of Representatives and the Senate (the two chambers of the United States Congress) agreed on a sanctions package. The bill had several minor provisions: to stop the import of Krugerrands; forbid the sale of American nuclear equipment; prohibit loans to the South African government and its corporations unless these were to be used for social services open to blacks as well as whites; and prevent the sale of computers to state agencies enforcing apartheid legislation. Much more important was its major provision: to ban new investment after a year unless there was significant progress towards ending apartheid. The progress would have to be evident in several areas, such as eliminating influx control, Group Areas restrictions, and forced removals; negotiating a new political system with truly representative black leaders; and freeing all political prisoners.[53]

On 1 August 1985, the House of Representatives passed the bill by a huge majority, 380 to 48. President Reagan viewed the development 'with a jaundiced eye', saying that sanctions 'would hurt the very people we wanted to help'.[54] This notwithstanding, the Senate seemed set to pass the bill in September, with a large enough majority to ensure that the President could be overridden if he exercised his right to veto the bill.

At that juncture Reagan was faced with the prospect of an embarrassing defeat for his policy of 'constructive engagement'. So on 9 September, the day before the Senate vote, Reagan reversed his opposition to sanctions, and as an executive measure announced his own more limited package. His purpose, he said, was 'to heal the debate in the United States and to send a unified signal to South Africa'.[55] The Republican majority in the Senate accepted his lead, and defeated several attempts by the Democrat minority to force a vote on the original bill.

Although seeming to bow to pressure, Reagan shrewdly pre-empted Congress with provisions that were significantly weaker in three respects. Firstly, the four minor proposals which he did incorporate from the Congress bill were nugatory: Krugerrand sales had fallen off to a trickle in any case, and the other restrictions had either been introduced previously or were already being voluntarily observed. Secondly, he entirely omitted the major proposal of the bill, the threat of banning new investment. Thirdly, the measure he inserted instead was itself deceptive. Export assistance was denied to any American company employing more than twenty-five people in South Africa but failing to adhere to the Sullivan code. However, the rendition of the code in Reagan's executive order omits the crucial clause by which the code was strengthened at the end of 1984, viz., the requirement that companies press for broad changes including the repeal of apartheid legislation.

The point is thus that the political measures in Reagan's package are not only very mild, but only there at all in order to head off economic sanctions. Dr Chester Crocker, Assistant Secretary of State for African Affairs, summarized it well: 'Our policy remains the same but we have added additional signals .... The measures selected represent political sanctions .... The President has no intention of adopting measures that would hurt or damage the South African economy.'[56]

Bishop Tutu's reaction was that President Reagan was 'bending over backwards to save the South African government from the consequences of its own actions'.[57] The UDF dismissed the package as another attempt 'to rescue the sinking apartheid ship'.[58] It would likewise be a severe disappointment to the strong majority sentiment in favour of disinvestment identified in our survey.

However dramatic the contest between Reagan and Congress, in its closing moments it was nearly upstaged on the South African scene by US bankers, who precipitated a loans crisis in August 1985. This achieved almost overnight the sort of impact, at least in the short term, for which the disinvestment lobby had been mobilizing all year.

The underlying cause of the crisis was the 'hidden time bomb'[59] described in the previous section: the 'foolish', 'profligate'[60] accumulation over the preceding few years, by the government and para-statal organizations as well as banks and companies,[61] of a huge foreign debt of $21-22bn, about half of which was short-term (including long-term debts maturing in the twelve months after August 1985).

Approximately one-fifth of the total amount was owed to banks in the United States. They had already been 'managing down' their involvement, in response to domestic divestment pressures from large depositors or shareholders like city authorities.[62] This policy was accelerated as bankers in the US viewed the saturation television coverage of the urban violence in South Africa, especially after the State of Emergency was declared in June. When the Chase Manhattan Bank decided not to participate in a South African company loan in July, the foreign exchange market teetered. It was toppled by President Botha's uncompromising response to the riots, in his first 'Rubicon' speech in August.[63] Dismayed, the remaining US banks refused in concert to extend their maturing loans. As the rand plummeted to

35 US cents, the South African government was forced to respond with alacrity. It closed the Stock Exchange for a day, temporarily suspended foreign exchange dealings, and announced a unilateral moratorium on repaying its short-term debt.

The former governor of the Reserve Bank immediately toured foreign capitals, and a Swiss financier was engaged to mediate between the overseas banks and the government.[64] The government also shrewdly imposed stringent controls on news coverage of the unrest, under the Emergency regulations. Foreign confidence gradually revived and took the rand back to 50 US cents early in 1986, easing the mediator's task.

In November 1985 and February 1986 the South African Council of Churches issued statements, signed by the General Secretary Dr Beyers Naudé, Bishop Tutu, and Dr Allan Boesak, appealing to the bankers to reject the rescheduling proposals unless the government resigned.[65] Similar appeals to the US banks were made by fifteen Congressmen, including the Speaker of the House of Representatives, and by the heads of twenty American church groups.[66]

But the European and American bankers ignored the calls, and in February 1986 an agreement in principle was reached governing the repayment or rescheduling of the debt.[67] Indeed, the mediator had made clear at the outset that, like President Reagan, he was absolutely opposed to economic sanctions because he believed the economically less-favoured majority would suffer most from them.[68] The South African authorities saw the agreement as paving the way for their return to international credit markets, although they reckoned that the way would be a long, hard one.[69] Their caution was appropriate. In the actual implementation of the agreement, some banks insisted that certain payments which were to have been made in regular quarterly instalments be brought forward to the start of the scheme.[70] The feeling that the Reserve Bank would have difficulty in finding the hefty lump sum of $430 million by mid-April pushed the rand back below 50 US cents.[71]

At about the same time, there were indications in the United States that the apartheid issue was coming back to the boil. Organized labour joined a campaign to get Royal Dutch Shell to cut trade with South Africa; a New York City fund planned shareholder action to prohibit Mobil selling oil to the South African government; and protests began to take place again on many American campuses, including violent confrontations among students and with the police about the construction of shanty-towns symbolizing living conditions under apartheid.[72]

It might have seemed that President Reagan was mindful of these renewed pressures when, at the end of March 1986, he announced that the economic sanctions he instituted six months before should remain in force because South Africa's racial segregation policies continued to pose 'an unusual and extraordinary threat' to the foreign policy and economy of the United States. However, his announcement was actually the outcome of a routine periodical assessment stipulated in his original sanctions order.[73]

Much more to the point was the reaction of the US government to Bishop Tutu in April. The Bishop had issued a major statement: 'Our children are dying. Our land is burning and bleeding and so I call the international community to apply punitive sanctions against this government to help us establish a new South Africa [that is] non-racial, democratic, participatory and just.' A US Democratic Congressman heeded the plea and prepared to move a prohibition on US investment in South Africa, as well as the much more dramatic measure of a total ban on the import and export of goods and information between the two countries.[74] The US State Department replied that sanctions would hurt South Africa's economy, which was central to the region's stability and a major force for change within the country. A more telling justification was added by Dr Crocker: 'The ban would unnecessarily preclude access to South African minerals and resources, some of which are significant to our national security.'[75]

Now some 20% of all direct foreign investment in South Africa comes from the United States. But, given the huge size of the American economy, this amounts to only 1% of American investment abroad. So the US could afford, more than most, to use investment as a lever. Britain accounts for 50% of foreign investment in South Africa. And this amounts to fully 10% of British investment abroad.[76] This is a sizeable proportion. Britain's wariness to tamper with it became clear as, parallel to the American saga, the EEC (European Economic Community) countries evolved their sanctions policies.

After a three-day fact-finding visit to South Africa in August 1985, three European foreign ministers declared that they would not recommend economic sanctions to the EEC.[77] The EEC accordingly adopted a mixed package of measures. On the one hand, military attachés were to be recalled, and embargoes were placed on the export of arms, oil and 'sensitive' technology to South Africa. However — as with the Reagan package — most of these sanctions were already in effect. On the other hand, the EEC decided to beef up its code of conduct for companies operating in South Africa, to offer aid to non-violent oppositional organizations, to support educational programmes for blacks, and to break off official cultural, scientific and sporting relations with South Africa in favour of more contact with black South Africans.[78]

A couple of countries have gone further. Following the imposition of the State of Emergency in South Africa in July, the socialist French government jumped the gun on the EEC deliberations, and prohibited new investment.[79] The Netherlands and Denmark have done likewise, and a couple of smaller European countries have blocked export credits.[80]

At the other end of the spectrum the most defiantly conservative reaction came from the West German government. Foreign Minister Genscher was condemned for breaking off cultural relations in line with the EEC package. The centre-right coalition in Parliament instead passed a motion setting up cultural and sporting links with all racial groups, and affirmed its opposition to economic sanctions.[81]

Between the two extremes, the British government was reluctant to go as far as the EEC package, especially regarding the withdrawal of military attachés, and initially went along only with the 'positive' measures. However, what changed Mrs Thatcher's mind was the prospect of embarrassing pressure, both at the UN and at a forthcoming Commonwealth conference. At the latter Britain faced criticism from the 'white' Commonwealth countries, Canada, Australia and New Zealand, which had recently adopted sanctions packages,[82] and also the disapproval of important African trading partners.[83]

Significantly, in making her about-face on political and military sanctions Mrs Thatcher was as adamant as President Reagan that Britain still opposed economic sanctions and trade boycotts.[84] In a virtual echo of Reagan and Crocker, the British Ambassador to South Africa, Sir Patrick Moberley, said that 'the British government's decision is therefore intended as a political signal... but one which deliberately steers clear of hurting the economy and the lives of the people we are trying to help'.[85]

Outside the government in Britain, attitudes to disinvestment are more mixed. The Confederation of British Industry firmly supports Mrs Thatcher's approach, and claims that business is the most liberal element in South Africa, in cheerful disregard of the poor progress of British subsidiaries in South Africa towards de-segregation and reasonable wage levels,[86] which we noted above. By contrast, the Leader of the Opposition in the British Parliament, Neil Kinnock, has rejected constructive engagement, and promised that a Labour government will enforce sanctions.[87] When the loans crisis broke, he urged that the Bank of England should not help to bail the South African government out. Similar calls were made by the Liberal Party and the Social Democrats.[88] When the agreement to reschedule South Africa's foreign debt was reached, *The Observer* remarked that it bestowed 'an aura of sham respectability on a bloodstained regime ... aid to apartheid is wrong, whether it takes the form of bullets or bank loans'.[89]

This view is shared by the British Council of Churches. However, the stance of the Church of England is more equivocal. Its General Synod took a resolution supporting 'progressive disengagement' in 1982, and the Church does not invest directly in South Africa. But two-thirds of the British companies in which it has shares in turn have a stake in South Africa. And in February 1986 the Church Commissioners insisted that the Church would seriously damage its long-term interests if it sold its shares in those companies, though it obliges them to comply with the EEC code.[90]

With the establishment thus seeming to be firmly united against disinvestment, it came as a surprise when Barclays Bank in London announced in March 1986 that it would refuse to make any new loans or reschedule existing debts 'until there are changes which confirm an end to the bankrupt policy of institutionalised racial discrimination'.[91] The announcement was all the more surprising because financial commentators had intimated during the US loans crisis that European and British bankers viewed the US action as rather hysterical and were themselves far more sensible and sober about lending to South Africa.

However, the Thatcher government remained true to form, and were in accord with the Reagan Administration in their response to Bishop Tutu's call in April 1986 for punitive sanctions against the South African regime. A Foreign Office spokesman said that 'we continue to believe that such boycotts would only make matters worse'.[92]

The overall impact on South Africa of these constraints on foreign investments and loans has been undeniably important in one way, yet clearly restricted in another. The importance was cogently summarized by Harry Oppenheimer in March 1986. The loans crisis 'raised pressure on [South Africa] to a level never before experienced and demonstrated South Africa's vulnerability in our economically dependent world'; likewise, the advocacy of disinvestment by anti-apartheid groups and student activists 'could no longer be ignored'. These pressures were becoming powerful influences on the government's reform policies. In his view, the most serious pressure came from private institutions, such as banks, universities, unions, churches and corporations. But the sanctions introduced by the United States, European and Japanese governments, albeit mild, showed that 'opposition in principle to sanctions, as a means of effecting change in South African policies, has been breached'.[93]

On the other hand, the restriction in the impact of sanctions arises from the vast difference between what private institutions can do and what the various foreign governments will accede to. Our analysis in this section has displayed a clear pattern. Nearly all the major powers are still 'talking business' with South Africa.[94] Countries with little at stake are fairly ready to respond to the demands of black South African unions, churches and political movements for economic measures *in addition to* political ones. But the recalcitrants tend to be countries like Britain and West Germany,[95] with massive investments, conservative regimes, and every intention of staying. They are sending political 'signals' *instead of* undertaking economic sanctions. Bishop Tutu's criticism of the bankers appears to apply also to the key governments, that their interest is 'in profits, and not in people being shot, detained or resettled'.[96]

Notes

1 Lawrence Schlemmer, 'Black worker attitudes: political options, capitalism and investment in South Africa', Document and Memorandum Series of the Centre for Applied Social Sciences at the University of Natal, September 1984; 'Disinvestment: new research on black reactions in South Africa', *loc. cit.*, February 1985; 'Disinvestment and black worker attitudes in South Africa: rejoinder to critical comment by M.O. Sutcliffe and P.A. Wellings', *loc. cit.*, June 1985.

2 Schlemmer, 'Black worker attitudes: political options', *op. cit.*, p.36 and p.34; Schlemmer, 'Disinvestment: new research', *op. cit.*, p.12.

3 Chris de Kock et al., 'Volwasse Swartes in die Pretoria-Witwatersrand-Vaaldriehoekgebied se persepsies van ekonomiese boikotte teen Suid-Afrika: 'n vergelyking van drie opnames se gegewens', Human Sciences Research Council, Pretoria, mimeo, August 1985.

4 Peter Godwin and David Lipsey, 'Sanctions: black support grows', *Sunday Times* (London), 25 August 1985. For a local report see 'What blacks think', *The Sunday Star*, 25 August 1985.

5 Lindsey Gruson, 'US minister says his code can be a crowbar to change South Africa', *International Herald Tribune*, 18 September 1985. See also *Race Relations Survey 1984* (Johannesburg: SA Institute of Race Relations, 1985), p.862.

6 *Race Relations Survey 1984* (Johannesburg: SA Institute of Race Relations, 1985), p.916. For a more recent statement see Carol Lazar, 'A day in the life of Tutu', *The Sunday Star*, 10 November 1985.

7 'FOSATU international policy statement, April 1984' and 'CUSA statement on the Kennedy visit', *SA Labour Bulletin*, 10:6 (May 1985), 44-46. Upon its formal inception in December 1985 the new 500 000-strong Congress of South African Trade Unions (COSATU) – which includes most of the unions formerly in FOSATU, many previously un-affiliated unions, and the National Union of Mineworkers which was previously affiliated to CUSA – made it clear that it supported the threat of disinvestment 'as an essential and effective form of pressure on the South African regime'. See 'Sanctions call meets widespread opposition', *The Star*, 4 April 1986.

8 Estelle Trengove, 'SACC backs disinvestment in resolution', *The Star*, 28 June 1985; Nat Diseko, 'Hit SA harder – SACC', *The Star*, 30 June 1985.

9 It has been suggested that the intermediate option could as well have been labelled 'conditional investment', so that the results could be interpreted as showing that some seventy-five per cent of respondents actually favoured some or other form of *investment*. However, as the wording of the question makes clear, the intermediate option

proposes a move 'to *limit or restrict* investment', i.e. a change *away* from the previously prevailing situation in which investment was unrestricted and encouraged, and *towards*, though not as far as, total disinvestment. Our interpretation — that for summary purposes conditional disinvestment should be linked to total disinvestment rather than free investment — is corroborated by respondents' answers to a separate question, covered in Chapter 3. Some seventy per cent favoured pressures on businessmen to demand changes from the government, i.e. only thirty per cent favoured businessmen being left to their business without constraint.

10 Professor L. Schlemmer, 'The report on the attitude surveys', Chapter 3 in *The Buthelezi Commission*, Vol. I (Durban: H + H Publications, ?1982), p.190.

11 *Ibid.*, p.189.

12 David Allen, 'When disinvestment will hit whites', *The Sunday Star*, 9 June 1985.

13 Lawrence Schlemmer, 'Black worker attitudes: political options', *op. cit.*, p.37.

14 Lawrence Schlemmer, 'Disinvestment: new research', *op. cit.*, p.3, and 'Disinvestment and black worker attitudes in South Africa: rejoinder', *op. cit.*, p.12.

15 Lawrence Schlemmer, 'The dynamics of sanctions', *op. cit.*, p.43, and 'Disinvestment: consequences and black reactions in South Africa', mimeo, no date, p.5.

16 Phillip van Niekerk, 'Most blacks want sanctions, poll shows', *Weekly Mail*, 13-19 September 1985; Lawrence Schlemmer, 'Were we really polls apart?', *Sunday Times*, 15 September 1985.

17 Phillip van Niekerk, 'Most blacks want sanctions', *op. cit.*

18 'What blacks think', *The Sunday Star*, 25 August 1985.

19 Mangosuthu G. Buthelezi, 'Inkatha says no', *Leadership* (June 1985), 66-68 (p.66) and 'It's now the democratic process versus violence', *The Star*, 30 January 1986.

20 'Pleas for non-violent change are met with more oppression — Tutu', *The Star*, 24 January 1986.

21 Jon Qwelane, 'Sanctions without shedding one tear', *The Sunday Star*, 6 April 1986. For an almost identical argument, see the statement by Cyril Ramaphosa, General Secretary of the National Union of Mineworkers, in 'Oppenheimer warns US on sanctions', *The Star*, 21 March 1985.

22 Lawrence Schlemmer, 'The dynamics of sanctions', *Leadership* (June 1985), 39-43 (p.43).

23 'Independent churches "silent for too long"', *The Star*, 8 November 1985; 'Apartheid: AFM states its position', *The Star*, 22 March 1986.

24 'Anti-apartheid lobbyists pile on pressure', *Computer Week*, 25 March 1985.

25 Michael Holman and Jim Jones, 'Sanctions: UK has most to lose', *The Star*, 10 August 1985.

26 *Race Relations Survey 1984* (Johannesburg: SA Institute of Race Relations, 1985), p.862.

27 'FOSATU international policy statement, April 1984', *SA Labour Bulletin*, 10:6 (May 1985), p.44; 'No simple equation: local response to disinvestment', *Work in Progress*, 37 (June 1985), 18-21; 'Company assets belong in SA', *The Star*, 12 December 1985.

28 Stephen Gelb, 'Unemployment and the disinvestment debate', *SA Labour Bulletin*, 10:6 (May 1985), 54-66.

29 *Ibid.*, p.56. See also 'GM invests R40m in new production line', *Business Day*, 22 March 1985 and 'Temporary layoffs at GM', *The Star*, 22 March 1985.

30 M.O. Sutcliffe and P.A. Wellings, 'Disinvestment and black worker "attitudes" in South Africa: a critical comment', forthcoming in *Review of African Political Economy*. Unionists have also made the point: see the comment by the treasurer of the Metal and Allied Workers Union, Maxwell Xulu, in 'Company assets belong in SA', *The Star*, 12 December 1985.

31 Deborah Derrick, 'Sanctions: a third option', Woodrow Wilson School of International Relations, Princeton University, mimeo, 28 August 1985.
32 *Race Relations Survey 1984* (Johannesburg: SA Institute of Race Relations, 1985), pp.276-290.
33 Deborah Derrick, *op. cit.*, p.14. Interestingly, the same sort of approximation — though only in respect of black workers — has been made by a prominent Johannesburg stockbroker, Max Borkum, in arguing that disinvestment would actually benefit the South African economy: 'SA stands to gain if US firms pull out', *Business Day*, 5 June 1985.
34 'Selective sanctions are SA's only hope', *The Star*, 3 October 1985.
35 See notes 20 and 21 above.
36 Howard Preece, 'The reality of disinvestment', *Rand Daily Mail*, 15 March 1985.
37 Patricia Cheyney, 'US pull-out inevitable — magazine', *Sunday Times*, 15 September 1985. See also 'US firms stand firm against disinvestment', *Computer Week*, 25 March 1985.
38 'SA "no longer an attractive place to do business" say US companies', *The Star*, 13 September 1985; 'Investment "cut by R2,6bn"', *The Star*, 10 April 1986.
39 'Activists launch anti-SA letter', *The Star*, 27 September 1985. See also 'Money crisis was a hidden time bomb', *The Citizen*, 9 September 1985.
40 'De Kock seeks help of US banks to stem cash drain', *The Citizen*, 31 August 1985.
41 'Transnational corporations and apartheid', a working paper of the SA Council of Churches, Division of Justice and Reconciliation, mimeo, 13 September 1985, pp.6-7; Derrick, *op. cit.*, p.9.
42 'Ignoring Sullivan', *Financial Mail*, 3 May 1985.
43 Derrick, *op. cit.*, p.21.
44 Sheryl Raine, 'Employment codes do not bring change, says the ILO', *The Star*, 1 October 1985.
45 Peter Mann, 'EEC squabbling over plan', *The Star*, 22 January 1986.
46 See, for example, 'Foreign pressure welcome — FOSATU', *City Press*, 5 May 1985.
47 Deborah Derrick, 'Sanctions: a third option', *op. cit.*, pp.19-22. See also Sheryl Raine, 'Employment codes do not bring change', *op. cit.*
48 Bernie Fanaroff, 'Transnationals and responsibility', *Financial Mail*, 1 October 1985.
49 'Universities change policy', *The Star*, 31 August 1985; 'Industrialists start to pull out of South Africa', *The Sunday Star*, 22 September 1985.
50 Peter Honey, 'Sanctions: South Africa will feel the pinch', *Business Day*, 27 September 1985; 'Industrialists start to pull out of South Africa', *op. cit.* Other prominent companies that have decided to disinvest since September 1985 include AT&T, the gigantic communications and computer conglomerate, Bell and Howell, and CBS Records.
51 Ramsay Milne, 'Phibro-Salomon's pull-out puts Oppenheimer in anomalous spot', *The Star*, 23 August 1985. See also 'SA "no longer an attractive place to do business" say US companies', *The Star*, 13 September 1985.
52 'US firms back lobby for reforms', *The Star*, 23 September 1985.
53 Hannes de Wet, 'Sanctions — a spectre that won't go away', *The Star*, 15 August 1985.
54 'Reagan casts "jaundiced eye" at sanctions', *The Star*, 26 August 1985.
55 'Reagan said "yes" to heal rift in US', *The Citizen*, 16 September 1985.
56 'Sanctions must not hurt SA — Crocker', *The Citizen*, 27 September 1985.
57 '"Congress influenced sanctions decision"', *The Star*, 10 September 1985.
58 'SA, rand get a breathing space', *The Star*, 10 September 1985.
59 'Money crisis was a hidden time bomb', *The Citizen*, 9 September 1985.
60 *The Economist*, quoted in 'Foreign bankers should press for change by backing SA business', *The Star*, 7 September 1985; 'Liberty Life Group: Statement by the Chairman, Mr Donald Gordon', *The Star*, 14 March 1986.

61 'Chances excellent of debts agreement', *The Citizen*, 12 September 1985.
62 'Swiss bankers are told to be cautious', *The Citizen*, 9 September 1985.
63 'De Kock in Zurich', *The Citizen*, 9 September 1985.
64 *Ibid.*; 'Leutwiler will quit if his mediation helps apartheid', *The Star*, 6 November 1985.
65 'Leutwiler will quit . . .', *op. cit.*; 'Banks only interested in profits, claims Tutu', *The Star*, 21 February 1986.
66 'US banks urged to put pressure on SA', *The Star*, 19 February 1986.
67 Neil Behrmann, 'It's a long, hard road back to normality − Stals', *The Star*, 21 February 1986.
68 'Leutwiler will quit . . .', *op. cit.*
69 'Banks only interested in profits . . .', *op. cit.*; Neil Behrmann, 'It's a long hard road . . .', *op. cit.*
70 'Banks accept 5% payment on debts', *The Star*, 17 March 1986.
71 Gareth Costa, 'Rand continues under pressure', *The Star*, 22 March 1986; Reg Rumney, 'Three factors behind the rand's latest dip', *Weekly Mail*, 27 March - 3 April 1986.
72 Alan Dunn, 'Boiling point nears again', *The Star*, 21 March 1986; 'Pressure on Mobil for oil ban', *The Star*, 18 March 1986; '88 arrested in anti-apartheid riot in US', *The Star*, 4 April 1986; 'Taste of apartheid for US students', *The Star*, 5 April 1986.
73 Neil Lurssen, 'Low-key Reagan springs a surprise', *The Star*, 20 March 1986.
74 Anton Harber, 'Tutu off to see "our friends" on sanctions', *Weekly Mail*, 4-10 April 1968; 'Reagan men oppose tougher SA sanctions', *The Star*, 10 April 1986.
75 'Bishop's plea rejected by US government', *The Star*, 3 April 1986; 'Reagan men oppose tougher SA sanctions', *op. cit.*
76 Peter Honey, 'Sanctions: South Africa will feel the pinch', *op. cit.* See also Michael Holman and Jim Jones, 'Sanctions: UK has most to lose', *op. cit.*
77 Sue Leeman, 'EEC Ministers will not call for disinvestment', *The Star*, 2 September 1985.
78 Peter Mann, 'EEC dumps SA whites', *Sunday Tribune*, 15 September 1985.
79 'SA embroiled in diplomatic rows with France, US', *Business Day*, 25 July 1985.
80 'EEC may decide on sanctions today', *The Star*, 10 September 1985.
81 'W Germany for greater links with all SA groups', *The Citizen*, 27 September 1985.
82 'Aussie strategy on SA', *The Star*, 1 October 1985; Nicholas Ashford, 'Sanctions, will the Iron Lady bend?', *The Star*, 15 October 1985; 'Canada imposes sanctions on SA', *The Star*, 14 September 1985.
83 'Embattled Thatcher stands by her policy despite Reagan move', *The Star*, 10 September 1985.
84 Colleen Ryan and David Braun, 'British sanctions seen as political signal', *The Star*, 26 September 1985.
85 'UK ambassador defends anti-SA moves', *The Citizen*, 27 September 1985. See also Richard Walker, 'A better part of valour . . .', *Business Day*, 27 September 1985.
86 'Companies can beat apartheid, say businessmen', *The Star*, 9 September 1985.
87 'Kinnock calls for action against SA', *The Star*, 24 July 1986.
88 'Kinnock calls for ban on financial aid to SA', *The Star*, 11 August 1985.
89 'UK paper condemns SA debt deal', *The Star*, 24 February 1986.
90 'Church will not break investment links with SA', *The Star*, 5 February 1986. See also 'Investing in SA a betrayal of the clergy − minister', *The Star*, 6 February 1986.
91 David Braun, 'Barclays decision "remarkable" − PFP', *The Star*, 7 March 1986.
92 'Sanctions call meets widespread protest', *The Star*, 4 April 1986.
93 'Oppenheimer: Threat of sanctions grows', *The Star*, 14 March 1986.

94 'EEC may decide on sanctions today', *The Star*, 10 September 1985.
95 Peter Mann, 'EEC squabbling over plan', *The Star*, 22 January 1986.
96 'Banks only interested in profits, claims Tutu', *The Star*, 21 February 1986.

Chapter 3

Urban Black Political Movements: Means and Ends

Violence: adjunct or alternative to disinvestment?

In the previous chapter, we have reported and interpreted aggregate indications of black attitudes towards different disinvestment strategies. However, disinvestment should not be considered in isolation from the socio-political milieu in which it arises. The major black political tendencies have adopted more or less explicit policies on the issue, significantly uniting some of them in this important respect and setting them against others. Also, disinvestment is one among a range of possible strategies, all directed towards bringing about a substantially different dispensation in South Africa. There are evocative patterns in blacks' attitudes to these strategies. By setting the issue of disinvestment in these contexts, we can discern which are and are not viable avenues of fundamental change.

Let us first consider the range of strategies for social change. In preparing our survey, we distinguished five major and distinct possibilities that were being discussed in the prevailing debate. We then asked respondents in each case whether they thought blacks were justified in using the strategy to press the government to change (Question 4 in the Appendix). Interestingly, the option of 'genuine negotiations between the government and true leaders of the black people' rated highest, receiving the assent of 90% of respondents, despite months of crisis in which several hundreds of blacks had been killed in confrontations with the police and several thousands detained without trial.

Next in popularity was the strategy of overseas pressure on businessmen to demand changes from the government, which received approval from more than two-thirds of respondents (70%). Direct actions by blacks within South Africa — such as strikes, boycotts of white businesses, and protests against high rents and unequal education — were regarded as justified by a similar proportion of the sample (66%).

Alongside these non-violent means of change, a sizeable minority of urban black South Africans would countenance violent means: more than a third (36%) approved armed struggle against the government's security forces, and more than a quarter (28%) regarded attacks on blacks who work for the system, such as community councillors and homelands authorities, as warranted.

These results have a chilling implication. Nearly all white leaders in business and government, many religious spokesmen, and some black leaders like Chief Buthelezi, have drawn a sharp distinction between non-violent political activities, which they regard as legitimate, and violent ones which they adamantly reject. The figures suggest that the distinction is not nearly so hard and fast for many blacks: while violence is rejected by roughly one-half of those who welcome pressure from abroad or strikes within, the other half regard it as a justifiable adjunct to peaceful strategies. One might surmise that the latter have come, through the teargas and shootings and detentions that are now everyday features of township life, to a gut understanding of Von Clausewitz's dictum that war is the continuation of politics by other means.

The minorities that are prepared to countenance violent tactics are consonant in size — between a quarter and a third of the sample — with those adopting a 'hard-line' position on disinvestment and on the risk of resulting unemployment. Indeed, there is a highly significant association between the respective positions. An appreciable minority of urban blacks evidently espouse a systematic and very militant anti-apartheid position, and regard violence as justified in their bitter determination to dismantle apartheid.

The leading black tendencies
At the same time, nearly everyone would still welcome negotiations. This underlines the importance of exploring the prerequisites of negotiation specified in our question, viz., who are regarded as the 'true leaders of the black people', and what would have to be involved for the process to be accepted as 'genuine'.

To give the issue of leadership a material context, respondents were presented with some preliminary questions. First they were asked how they felt about life in South Africa, and how they thought it was changing (Question 1 in the Appendix). Two-thirds were angry with the situation, and three-quarters thought it was deteriorating. To get a better feel of this fierce mood, we invited respondents, in an open-ended question, to give their 'main problems or grievances about how things are in South Africa today'. Grievances concerning political (29%), economic (29%), and welfare (20%) matters accounted for more than three-quarters of the replies. (More detailed categorizations are listed at Question 2 in the Appendix.) Only then came the police shootings, riots and detentions (11%), and finally education (8%) and other issues (3%). All the travail of the Emergency did not distract respondents from their demands for the basic rights of a vote, a job, and a home.

Respondents were then given another open choice, in answering 'which one leader or organization would you most like to represent you, in solving [your] problems or grievances?' (Question 3 in the Appendix). The detailed results and main categories are presented in Table 3, and Figure 3 overleaf usefully illustrates the latter. We find that Nelson Mandela and the ANC receive most votes, 31%, followed by Bishop Desmond Tutu with 16%. The UDF came next with 8%; and for the purpose of analysing

Table 3 Urban black support for major political tendencies: CASE/IBR, September 1985

Tendency	Subtotal %	Item %
Nelson Mandela & ANC	**31**	
Nelson Mandela		23
ANC		8
UDF & radical groups	**14**	
UDF		8
AZAPO/AZASM		1
Dr Allan Boesak		1
COSAS/AZASO		1
PAC		1
SACC		1
Trade unions		1
Bishop Desmond Tutu	**16**	16
Chief Buthelezi & Inkatha	**8**	
Chief Buthelezi		6
Inkatha		2
Government & pro-investment groupings	**8**	
PW Botha/government		5
Community councillors		2
White opposition		1
Sundry	**24**	
Don't know		8
Other		3
None/'no leader'		13
	101[a]	**101**[a] (n = 800)

[a] The percentages total more than one hundred per cent because of small rounding errors in the component scores.

disinvestment, we have grouped with the UDF the half dozen other pro-disinvestment radical groups — COSAS/AZASO, AZAPO/AZASM, the PAC, trade unions, the SACC, and supporters of Dr Allan Boesak — which each received approximately 1% of mentions. This aggregate category thus totals 14% of the sample.

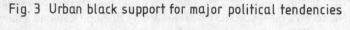

Fig. 3 Urban black support for major political tendencies

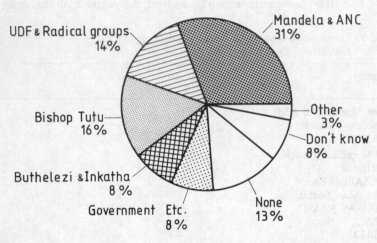

The pro-investment groupings which were mentioned, mainly the government and PW Botha, jointly score 8%. However, about a third of these respondents are indicating their assessment of the importance of such agencies rather than personal support, since they are also found to favour disinvestment and direct action to end apartheid in proportions similar to the rest of the sample.

The slice of the pie marked 'None' reflects the 13% of the sample who explicitly declined to answer the question, or insisted that there was no particular leader whom they looked to. The distribution of their answers to other important questions does not differ significantly from the sample average in each category. This fraction of respondents could thus be divided among the other tendencies according to the prevailing proportions, with no impact on the relative standing of the tendencies.

The remaining slices of the pie show the 8% who answered 'don't know', i.e., respondents who shrugged off the question; and the scattering of respondents who mentioned other tendencies, each of which was cited fewer than four times (less than half a per cent of the sample), to a total of 3%.

The overall pecking order which we found is well precedented in recent surveys of black attitudes. The only surprise in Figure 3 is that Chief Buthelezi (6%) and his Inkatha movement (2%) together achieve such a low level of aggregate support: less than a tenth of the urban black metropolitan vote. Once again, our result was reminiscent of one in the London *Sunday Times* study of a few weeks earlier. In their study, leaders had been separated from organizations by a question which asked respondents to choose from a list 'who would make the best President for South Africa'. Mandela polled 49%, Tutu 24%, and Buthelezi 6%.

The *Sunday Times* question was constructed differently from ours, and their sample did not include the Cape urban areas and Bloemfontein. So the actual percentages should not be compared. What is clearly similar is how far Buthelezi trails behind the top two choices. In earlier studies Buthelezi's support has been found to be much stronger, even across ethnic boundaries; and he is often described as the leader of the country's six million Zulus.[1] So the CASE/IBR result warrants more scrutiny.

Buthelezi's collapsing power-base

Let us first consider the changes over time in Buthelezi's following among all ethnic groups taken together, by contrast with the other major political tendencies. Table 4 compares data from the surveys by Hanf et al. in 1977 and by Schlemmer in 1981[2] with our own data in 1985. The comparison is slightly impressionistic, because the questions are not quite the same across all the studies; and comparable figures can only be extracted from the

Table 4 Support for political tendencies, by year (PWV region)

Tendency	Hanf et al. 1977 %	Schlemmer 1981 %	CASE/IBR 1985 %
Chief Buthelezi & Inkatha	28	17	5
Bishop Desmond Tutu	0	6	19
UDF & Radical groups[a]	16	9	13
Nelson Mandela & ANC	27	42	27
Sundry[b]	29	26	36
	100	100	100

[a] In 1977, this category included BC leaders and the PAC; in 1981, Dr Motlana and BC leaders; in 1985, the UDF, and other pro-disinvestment groupings.

[b] In 1977, this category included other homeland leaders (14%) and 'others/no answer' (15%); in 1981, homeland leaders (1%), non-South Africans (3%), diverse others (6%), and 'no answer' (16%); in 1985, the government (6%), diverse others (7%), 'nobody' (14%) and 'no answer' (9%).

published material on a regional basis. Even so, a clear pattern is evident.

The percentages in Table 4 cover the PWV metropolitan region. The trends are more conveniently seen in Figure 4, in which the 'sundry' category has been omitted for the sake of clarity. Over the period, Buthelezi's aggregate support in the PWV area (shown by the left-most set of pillars) dwindles steadily from 28% to 5%, while that of Bishop Tutu (shown by the next set of pillars) rises from 0% to 19%. In 1981 Buthelezi was well behind the ANC, but was still 'the most prominent internal leader figure' in this 'very important political arena', as Schlemmer noted at the time.[3] However, by 1985 Buthelezi's support in the arena is less than that of Tutu, as one sees by running one's eye across the front row of pillars. Buthelezi's showing here is also less than that of the UDF, even if one separates the UDF from the other radical groupings.

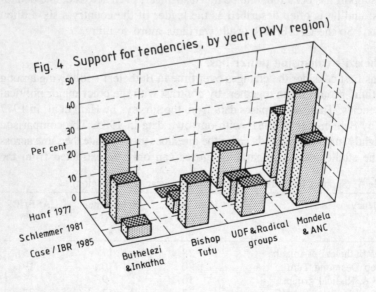

Fig. 4 Support for tendencies, by year (PWV region)

Figure 4 also shows that the base level of support for the ANC, which is 27% in 1977 and again in 1985, fluctuates upwards in 1981 at the expense of support for the other radical groupings, which dips for that year from 16% to 9%. The fluctuation probably reflects the initial impact of the enormous media coverage of the ANC after 1980, following the Free Mandela petition campaign and the very striking ANC assault on the government's SASOL petrol plant. Sundry remaining categories are differentiated in the footnote to Table 4.

A similar comparison for the Natal metropolitan region is shown in Table 5 and Figure 5. Buthelezi's vote in metropolitan Natal drops from three-quarters in 1977, through a half in 1981, to a third in 1985. In 1981,

Table 5 Support for political tendencies, by year (Natal region)

Tendency	Hanf et al.[a] 1977 %	Schlemmer 1981 %	CASE/IBR 1985 %
Chief Buthelezi & Inkatha	78	48	33
Bishop Desmond Tutu	0	5	9
UDF & Radical groups[b]	1	1	11
Nelson Mandela & ANC	8	26	21
Sundry[c]	13	20	26
	100	100	100

[a] Hanf's figures are for Durban Zulus. These may be a slight overestimate of Buthelezi support at the time among all ethnic groups in metropolitan Natal, to which the other two studies refer.

[b] In 1981, this included BC leaders; in 1985, the UDF, and other pro-disinvestment groupings.

[c] In 1981, this included homeland leaders (1%), non-South Africans (4%), diverse others (7%), and 'no answer' (8%); in 1985, the government (3%), diverse others (4%), 'nobody' (19%) and 'no answer' (3%).

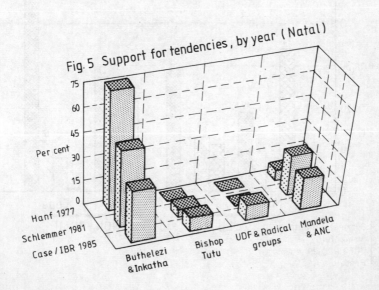

Fig. 5 Support for tendencies, by year (Natal)

many of the votes he lost went to the ANC, whereas following the inception of the UDF some of them went to that organization as well in 1985.
Bishop Tutu has steadily increased his support, as in the PWV.

One may even better understand the relationship between Buthelezi's support and that for the other major tendencies by breaking the figures down
not only by region, but also between Zulus and non-Zulus. This breakdown
is depicted in Figure 6. (Two clusters are omitted: there are too few non-
Zulus in the sample from metropolitan Natal to allow reliable analysis, and
there are almost no Zulus in the Cape regional sample. For the sake of
clarity, only the four major tendencies have been shown in each cluster.)
The actual percentages are listed above the respective columns. In each
cluster of columns, the support for Buthelezi is indicated by the column
on the extreme left; that for Bishop Tutu, and for the UDF and other radical groups, by the second and third columns; and that for Mandela and the
ANC by the column on the extreme right of the cluster.

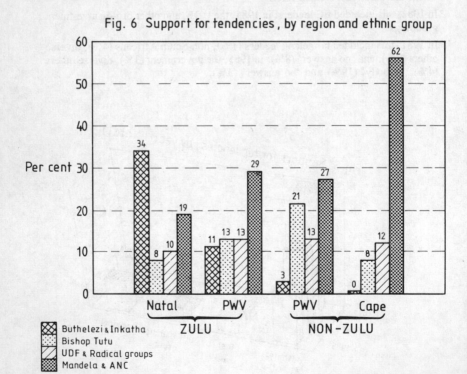

Fig. 6 Support for tendencies, by region and ethnic group

Consider the first cluster of columns, dealing with Zulu speakers in the urban Natal region. Buthelezi is clearly the single most popular choice, receiving 34% of their votes. However, as many are casting their votes for the other major tendencies taken together: 19% for the ANC plus 10% for the UDF etc., despite — or perhaps because of — the fact that Buthelezi has been linking these movements in his criticisms of them and declaring that they are at war with him;[4] plus 8% for Bishop Tutu, with whom Buthelezi has also been at odds.[5] So by 1985 Buthelezi is outnumbered in metropolitan Natal by three groupings which are effectively opposed to Inkatha and united in their support for the vision of the Freedom Charter, if not the means by which the ANC is pursuing it. Even in his heartland, Buthelezi's strategy of mobilizing politically along intra-black ethnic lines no longer appeals to a majority of Zulu speakers.

The role of urbanization in this erosion of Buthelezi's power-base becomes evident with the second set of columns, dealing with Zulus in the PWV area. They indicate that as one moves away from Natal, Buthelezi cannot safely claim to speak even for Zulus: his showing among them in the PWV falls to a tenth, as against a quarter for the ANC. The wide difference in his support in the respective regions is probably partly because Inkatha in the PWV does not have the patronage to dispense which it has in Natal; and partly because urban townships 'are melting-pots, in which individuals do not so much belong to different black peoples as merge into one black people'.[6]

Among non-Zulus in the PWV, depicted by the third cluster of columns, the ANC wins a quarter of the vote. This is the same as its showing among Zulus in the area, indicating that its support cuts across ethnic lines; whereas Buthelezi's clearly does not, since his vote in this cluster drops to a few per cent.

The contrast between Buthelezi and the ANC is completed in the fourth cluster of columns, reflecting non-Zulus in the Eastern and Western Cape, where Buthelezi's vote has dropped to zero, while the ANC's has risen to a massive 62%.

It emerges from this breakdown of our 1985 data that there are strong regional as well as ethnic effects at work. Buthelezi's showing among urban blacks diminishes, while that of the ANC increases, as one moves out of the Natal region and the Zulu-speaking group. Both effects pose problems for Buthelezi. Regionally, his attraction is weakest, and that of the ANC strongest, in the more populous areas. Ethnically, among urban dwellers, his laager largely keeps non-Zulus out, whereas it by now keeps only a minority of Zulus in. In conjunction, these processes largely explain the time trends displayed previously in Figures 4 and 5.

A further part of the explanation of the trends involves the way support for the various tendencies varies with age. Let us divide the sample into four categories: the youthful (16-24 years), the young (25-34), the middle-aged (35-50), and the old (50+). This allows us conveniently to report a remarkable and revealing pattern. The ANC's support is statistically indistinguishable across all the categories. This is a measure of its ongoing strength. Bishop Tutu's level of support among the middle-aged is slightly higher than his average level. The UDF's support is much greater among the youthful, and rather less among the old. And Buthelezi's is greater than average among the old, which is by far the least numerous category (because the average age of mortality for blacks is still well short of three-score and ten years). To put it rather literally, Buthelezi's likeliest adherents are dying, whereas the UDF's are still growing.

In sum, across the metropolitan areas of South Africa Buthelezi has basically lost the battle for popular support, and the decline in his showing can be expected to continue. This fact wreaks havoc with prognostications in the literature. Back in 1977, Hanf and his associates concluded from their survey figures that 'Buthelezi is undoubtedly the leader of his own group, but ... the support he enjoys goes far beyond it'. Neither proposition obtains any longer. In 1981, Schlemmer surmised that 'the position of Chief Buthelezi is fairly unassailable in KwaZulu and Natal, although the symbolic ANC leadership has made very considerable advances in urban areas'.[7] The latter clause of his analysis has weathered well, at the expense of the former.

It may be remarked that in contrasting Zulu with non-Zulu speakers we have not differentiated the latter. This simplification turns out to be justifiable, since the data confirm that Buthelezi pays for his support's being higher than average among Zulus by its being lower than average not only among Xhosas (where the ANC and Bishop Tutu do especially well), but also among Sothos and Tswanas.

Other differences amongst the tendencies are more subtle. For example, whereas Buthelezi adherents tend to be older, blue collar, less educated, and less frequent readers of newspapers than the average, adherents of the UDF tend to have post-secondary education, be students or white collar workers, read a newspaper daily, and belong to some or other voluntary organization. Social class rather than ethnicity is evidently at work here.

The remaining point to note from Figure 6 is that the level of support for the UDF and related anti-investment tendencies is remarkably consistent, across the various regions (including Natal, where their showing is unaffected by Buthelezi's vigorous condemnation) as well as the Zulu/non-Zulu ethnic boundary. Bishop Tutu's support, by contrast, peaks in the PWV region, where he is best known — previously as General Secretary of the SACC and subsequently as Bishop of Johannesburg. Because the PWV is by far the most populous region, this peak enhances his aggregate showing.

It is worth recalling at this juncture that our enquiry, like the disinvestment studies of Schlemmer and the HSRC, focusses on blacks resident in the major metropolitan areas. This is partly because it would have taken much longer and cost much more to try and cover rural areas systematically, and partly because it is the influential leaders and tendencies in the urban areas which mainly set the pace in black politics. But it is worth speculating on how the leadership rankings might have been affected by including rural as well as urban respondents in the sample. In particular, might there not then have been more overall support for Buthelezi, who is the only homeland leader to figure appreciably in the national ratings for urban areas?

It is undoubtedly true that Buthelezi's support *in KwaZulu* is higher in rural than in urban areas,[8] and the fall-off in his support over the last eight years may not have been as dramatic in the former as we have seen it to be in the latter. However, it is highly unlikely that Buthelezi's aggregate *national* popularity would be augmented much by support from the rural parts of the *other* homelands.

People in these other areas who display ethnic or regional loyalties — whether for traditional reasons or for the benefits which the authorities can deliver — will look to their own homeland leaders, rather than risk domination by the very large Zulu group. Conversely, those rurals who do temper their local orientation with a broader perspective will be less comfortable in turning to Buthelezi and Inkatha, which carry the taint of ethnic exclusivism, than to widely known, historically pan-black, political movements such as the ANC or PAC. The latter movements can accordingly expect a measure of support from the rural areas of each of the homelands, which will therefore sustain their overall rating.

How big might that measure be? As an indication, the Buthelezi Commission found that the proportion of support for the ANC among its respondents was about a quarter in the small towns of KwaZulu/Natal, and about a fifth in the rural areas.[9] On our argument, the ANC might expect to attract a similar order of support in any other homeland, whereas much of the balance of the vote would go to the local leader there rather than to Buthelezi.

In sum, the net effect on leadership ratings of including rural areas in the national sample would probably be that the ANC proportion holds roughly constant, while a couple of other homeland names make the list with a smattering of percentage points at the expense of Buthelezi and perhaps the radical groups.

There is some indirect empirical support for this deduction in our own sample, when one contrasts very urbanized respondents, who have lived in metropolitan areas for longer than twenty years, with those who have lived there for less, in respect of their leadership choices. Among the latter, i.e. the *less* urbanized, support for Mandela and the ANC is appreciably higher than the category average, whereas for Bishop Tutu it is slightly lower. Interestingly, the distribution of support for Buthelezi (and also for the UDF) does not differ from the average as between more and less urbanized respondents. These associations thus support our surmise that if any of the major tendencies stands to hold or even improve its position by the sampling of rural as well as metropolitan areas, it is the ANC rather than Buthelezi.

The motif in the mosaic: strategies and alignments

We have examined above the ways in which urban blacks regard disinvestment and other strategies of social change on the one hand, and the major urban black political tendencies on the other. We are now in a position to consider the association between the two. This will show how the issue of economic sanctions importantly unites some parties and sets them against others, and how similarities and differences regarding the other strategies constitute the parties' respective policy positions.

The strong relationship between disinvestment and political outlook is demonstrated in Figure 7. The columns depict the major political tendencies, arranged in ascending order of popular support. The shading within each column indicates how the adherents to the particular tendency divide up on the issue of disinvestment. The left-most column covers supporters of Buthelezi and Inkatha. It shows that an overwhelming majority of them, some three-quarters, support free investment. By contrast, in the remaining three columns, which correspond to the UDF et al., Tutu, and the ANC, the proportion in favour of free investment is less than a quarter, and as low as 10% in the case of the ANC.

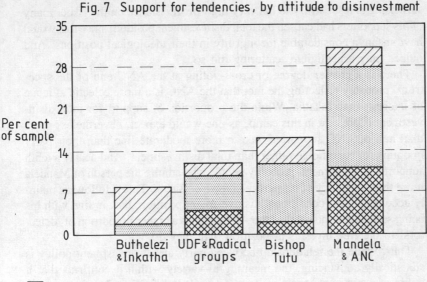

Fig. 7 Support for tendencies, by attitude to disinvestment

This pattern has three implications. Firstly, there is a clear divide between Buthelezi and the other three major tendencies, here being manifested by the disinvestment issue. And, secondly, the more popular the particular movement, the greater the support for one or other form of disinvestment. Indeed, one could frame an even stronger generalization, that the more popular the movement the greater the support for *total* disinvestment, were it not for the exception — conveyed by the shading within the third column of the figure — that Tutu's supporters so strongly favour conditional disinvestment. Thirdly, although the association between disinvestment and political tendency is strong, it is not perfect. There is quite a lot of 'cross-voting', in which people who chose in a particular way on the leadership question do not choose in the corresponding way on the disinvestment question, despite the leadership indications included as context in the latter.

Had the cross-voting been entirely random, it would have reflected ignorance or confusion among the respondents. But it displays an intuitively plausible pattern. For cxample, while most of Buthelezi's supporters accord with his position on free investment, a quarter nevertheless opt for conditional disinvestment: possibly active trade union members responding to the pull of a separate institutional affiliation. What would have been surprising is if, contrary to his very high-profile stance on the issue, many of his supporters had chosen the total disinvestment position, since this would have meant a considerable incongruity in their ideological positions. And indeed only a negligible scattering did so.

There is a greater degree of cross-voting at the ANC end of the spectrum, probably reflecting the fact that the ANC is a more eclectic alliance of interests than Inkatha. While the proportion of support for total disinvestment is greatest in this camp, as one would expect, nevertheless more than half of ANC supporters take a more moderate line than their party in opting for conditional rather than total disinvestment. And nearly a tenth support free investment, probably people who admire the person of Mandela more than the policy of his party. Likewise, Bishop Tutu's followers mainly accord with his conditional disinvestment position; but, in line with his being seen as less radical than the ANC, he has a higher proportion of 'defectors' to the free investment position than they do.

Thus, while the relationship between party and disinvestment policy is statistically convincing, the meaningful variety within it confirms that it holds as a matter of empirical fact rather than definition. In other words, our respondents are decision-takers rather than zombies, reasonably predictable in the aggregate because of the working of social forces, but richly variable as individuals because of the particular ways their respective biographies modulate the social context.

How does support for economic sanctions compare to support for the other strategies of social change amongst the different tendencies? In Figure 8, each row of pillars relates to a particular strategy, with each pillar indicating the proportion of respondents in the respective tendency who regard the use of the strategy as justified — from Buthelezi on the left of the diagram, through Bishop Tutu, then the UDF plus other pro-disinvestment groups, to the ANC on the right of the diagram. The tendencies have been displayed in order of increasing radicalism, rather than popularity, for a reason which will become evident below.

The rear row of pillars deal with peaceful negotiation. They are the same height, showing that the tendencies are indistinguishable in their readiness to entertain the 'motherhood and apple-pie' option of peaceful negotiation. But now consider the next two rows of pillars concerning direct action, whether external in the form of economic pressure or internal in the form of strikes, boycotts and protests. One sees again the divide which we identified above. Buthelezi's adherents (indicated by the left-most pillars) are much less prepared to support these activities than the adherents of the remaining major tendencies. The latter — supporters of the UDF plus other

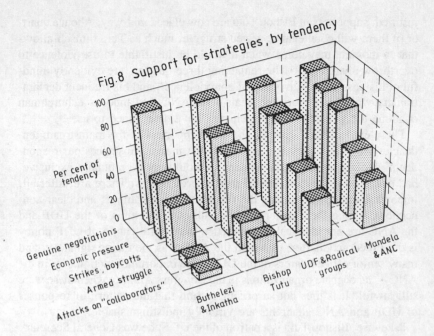

Fig.8 Support for strategies, by tendency

pro-disinvestment factions, of Bishop Tutu, and of the ANC plus Nelson Mandela — evidently constitute the urban black political mainstream in their largely similar responses to the important issues.

For example, a clear majority in each of the other three mainstream tendencies regard strikes etc. as justified: two-thirds in the case of Tutu and some four-fifths in the case of the UDF and the ANC. But only a minority, about a third, of Buthelezi supporters are keen on this form of action. The relative proportions are similar as regards support for economic sanctions. One can now understand the popularity of Buthelezi among businessmen, especially in Natal. As we saw earlier, his support among urban blacks there rises to a third. And Figure 8 displays how that third will tend to constitute a conciliatory and strike-free work-force.

The patterns are similar, but slightly more intricate, as regards the front two rows of pillars in Figure 8, depicting the two violent options of armed struggle and attacks on collaborators. Among supporters of the ANC and the radical groupings there is appreciable support for these options: for example, more than a half support armed struggle. By contrast, the proportion is negligible, less than a tenth, in Buthelezi's camp. So the divide exists here too. But in the extent to which they regard these strategies as justified, supporters of Bishop Tutu are now placed mid-way. About a quarter of them will countenance armed struggle, much as Tutu himself allows that 'a moment may come when it would be justifiable to use violence to overthrow apartheid'.[10] The remaining three-quarters are evidently mindful of his passionate 'advocacy of non-violence', and his frequent declaration that while he supports the ideals of the ANC, he cannot as a churchman condone the violent means which they have determined to use.[11]

These evident similarities in the way supporters of the mainstream tendencies view the policy issues suggest that in many instances our respondents' choices among these tendencies would not be mutually exclusive, had our survey question elicited further preferences. There are, after all, important similarities among the respective organizations, and clear connections among their leadership. So, although the aims of the UDF and the ANC are not identical,[12] in practice the central canon of UDF policy is the Freedom Charter, of which the ANC was the major signatory; and many senior office-bearers of the UDF were important functionaries in the ANC or its cognate organizations in the Congress Alliance when these were still lawful. It is thus not surprising to find that the pattern of responses of UDF and ANC adherents are virtually indistinguishable.

Likewise, Bishop Tutu is a patron of the UDF; he was General Secretary of the SACC and a patron of the National Forum, both of which are included alongside the UDF as pro-disinvestment organizations in our analysis; and he has lately called for Western leaders to side with the ANC, which, as he put it, 'sought to change an unjust system peacefully, non-violently, [until] they were sent into the arms of the struggle through violence because the West abandoned us'.[13] Our finding, that the pattern of policy responses of people in his camp is generally similar to that in the UDF and ANC, thus seems apt; as does the reservation that his followers are marginally more moderate on each issue, and especially on the question of violence.

In sum, the indications are that many of the black South Africans who specify their first preferences for Bishop Tutu, the UDF, and the other radical groupings (or at least the Charterist organizations among them such as AZASO and COSAS), would swing behind the most popular tendency, the ANC, if it were unbanned and free to campaign.

These data also have a more general implication. In the order in which they have been organized in the diagram, they graphically display a topography of attitudes: the more ideologically radical the party, the greater the proportion of its adherents prepared to countenance the more militant policy measures. This may seem to be a tautology, a typical instance of sociology's elaborately quantifying what one already knows. But it is actually an important empirical vindication of the remarkable discernment with which followers, many of them semi-literate, identify the positions of the important black political leaders whom they choose to support. In other words, black political culture in South Africa is detailed and sophisticated. It is also sensitively but steadily responsive to changing circumstances, as we saw in the third section of Chapter 2 on disinvestment, and in the previous section of this chapter on leadership. Given the long history of active black politics in South Africa one should not have expected otherwise, but for the readiness of some ostensibly informed white commentators to dismiss black political sentiments and strategies with notions like 'bombast' and 'freelance violence'.[14]

In noting the consonance between urban blacks' policy positions and their party affiliations, we have not yet sought to distinguish which causes which. People may have had some prior reason on the basis of which they chose a particular tendency. Conversely, they may have moved from an inchoate identification with a tendency to becoming more aware of its policies, and espousing them. Even in contexts like Britain where there is a highly educated and media-conscious electorate, and policy options are freely and widely disseminated, most people vote on grounds of party, or else personality, before policy. But this is at least in part because the class structure there is so firmly congealed, and so strongly aligned with the historically established, predominantly two-party system. It may be that in contemporary South Africa — where the political process for blacks is much less institutionalized, where the political atmosphere is highly charged by savage present repression and the prospect of fundamental future change, and where social movements are vying actively for recruits — black people are increasingly voting for a party because of their adherence to a policy rather than the other way round. Further multivariate analysis will be of considerable interest in clarifying the causal configurations for respondents in various demographic categories, and for the different movements.

Socialism in one state
We discovered in the previous section that the results revealed an ideological coherence within the urban black political mainstream, and a sharp contrast between the mainstream and Buthelezi. This model is given extra substance by our findings dealing with options for the future of South Africa.

As regards the *political* future, we followed our approach in the disinvestment question by staying close to the current debate between the prominent tendencies, rather than imposing our own abstract categorizations. The debate has increasingly been focusing on federalism. This is a central plank of Progressive Federal Party policy, as the name of the party indicates. During 1983, homeland leaders held a number of meetings to discuss forming a federation (in which regions have appreciable autonomy but nevertheless comprise a single political entity), in order to block Pretoria's intended confederation (a constellation of so-called independent states).[15] In 1984, Chief Buthelezi first declared that his Inkatha movement would accept power sharing in a federal system as a transitionary measure, in order to allay white fears about majority rule.[16] In mid-1985 Harry Oppenheimer canvassed the federal option.[17] On behalf of its business constituency, the Urban Foundation announced its support for a federal dispensation soon after.[18] Even Alan Paton announced that he had 'come to believe that Federation is the only possible form of constitution that holds any hope for the country'.[19] And in September 1985, in his speeches to the congresses of the provincial National Parties, PW Botha began to lead Nationalist opinion away from confederalism towards federalism, although he still avoided actually using the latter term.[20]

We accordingly offered respondents a choice between the kind of federal arrangement being bruited by the above parties, 'in which Africans are partly governed by homeland leaders but also have some representation in the central government', and a 'unitary arrangement in which all blacks and whites together vote for their leaders, to participate without regard to race or group in one central government for South Africa', of the kind proposed by AZAPO, UDF, PAC and ANC. As with the disinvestment issue, we sought to approximate to the circumstances surrounding a referendum or election by mentioning the tendencies in the formulation (see Question 8 in the Appendix).

On the basis of the sample, only one-fifth, 20%, of urban blacks will accept the federal compromise, while the remaining four-fifths, 80%, are holding out for a unitary non-racial democracy.

Broken down by political tendency, the proportion in favour of the unitary option among supporters of the ANC and Mandela was 94%; the UDF and the radical groups, 90%; and Bishop Tutu, 84%. In contrast with these very high figures, the proportion in favour of the federal option among supporters of Buthelezi and Inkatha was 62%. So one sees that the federal option does comparatively poorly overall partly because the fraction voting against the party 'line' as indicated in the question is much larger in the Buthelezi camp than in the others. At the same time, that the federal option achieves higher support from the whole sample than does Buthelezi suggests that appreciably more urban blacks are prepared, say, to try and allay white fears than are prepared to support Buthelezi's way of doing so.

The other differences between the two camps on this question are as revealingly clear cut. The statistical tests show that the minority prepared to accept federation tend to be older, less educated, Zulu-speaking, resident in Natal, and proponents of investment. On the other hand, support for the policy of one-person, one-vote, in one state was higher than average among the young, the better educated, non-Zulu speakers, residents of the PWV, and proponents of conditional or total disinvestment.

In other words, the deep schism between urban supporters of Buthelezi and the black political mainstream on the issue of the future political dispensation is the same as the schism we identified earlier regarding strategies for change.

Would rural respondents have been more conservative than our metropolitan sample on this matter? The answer is probably that they would have been, but much less so than might be expected. One can get some pointers from Schlemmer's 1981 survey for the Buthelezi Commission, which did have a rural component in its samples.[21]

On questions about the national political dispensation there was a negligible difference between urban and rural opinion. For example, Schlemmer's respondents were offered the black majority-rule option of 'one South African Parliament where the largest group in government, the blacks, have the power to make decisions for everyone'. The proportions declaring themselves 'happy' with this option in metropolitan versus rural areas of KwaZulu/Natal were very similar: 60% and 55% respectively. Even on questions of regional arrangements, in which rural respondents may have a greater potential interest at stake, the difference was negligible if the question was framed in the large. For example, only 32% of metropolitan respondents and 35% of rural respondents were 'happy' with what is now called the KwaNatal option, i.e., 'Natal and KwaZulu coming together so that black, white, Indian and Coloured can make many of their own laws for themselves in Natal and KwaZulu'. (This is precisely the sort of dispensation dear to Buthelezi's heart. It is therefore especially notable that his own Commission found only a minority actively supporting the idea itself, in rural or urban areas.)

Only with the explicit invocation of leadership, of the kind that is markedly more respected in the rural than the urban areas, did differences open up. For example, 29% of metropolitan respondents compared to 57% of rural ones were happy with 'homeland leaders and black township councillors sitting on a council with the white cabinet and so having some power over laws and policy'.

Now the form of the CASE/IBR question lies somewhere between the above poles. It deals with unitary versus federal arrangements in the large, on which one would expect little urban/rural difference. But in delineating the federal arrangement it adduces the role of local leadership, on which a difference may open up. On balance one might estimate that, had our overall sample covered the rural as well as the urban half of the population, the level of support for the federal option would indeed have been slightly larger than the 20% we found, but not nearly large enough to swing the overall majority away from the unitary option.

Let us now turn to the survey question on the *economic* future of the country. This issue is still largely hypothetical in South African popular debate. So we here accepted the approach of previous studies and for the sake of simplicity posed a basic opposition. As we defined it, the contrast was between socialism, in which workers have a say in the ownership and control of production, and capitalism, in which these are private (Question 9 in the Appendix). More than three-quarters, 77%, favoured the socialist vision, and less than one-quarter, 22%, the capitalist.

This majority is as decisive as that rejecting federalism. In this case, however, the distribution of opinion holds roughly constant across the categories of age, education, sex, and language, and even across the different political tendencies. Indeed, this is one respect in which Buthelezi is out of touch with the popular views he professes to articulate. He has, increasingly explicitly of late, pronounced in favour of the free enterprise system.[22] However, 70% of his declared urban followers favour socialism, a statistic only marginally — and not significantly — lower than the national average.

The only demographic factor which was statistically significant on this question was regional: support for socialism was markedly higher, 90%, in the Eastern Cape, which is the ANC heartland and the area where consumer boycotts have been most lasting and effective. And the only significant attitudinal association was with disinvestment: supporters of total disinvestment were more likely than the overall average to be inclined towards socialism (85%), and supporters of free investment rather less (72%). These are the sort of particular findings which, although more detailed than one would have hypothesised in advance, make persuasive sense when they emerge. They enhance one's confidence that respondents had a workable grasp of the implications of the economic issue, even though it was abstract.

Notes
1 For example, Hugh Murray, 'Publisher's notes', *Leadership* (June 1985), 5-7 (p.7).

2 Theo Hanf et al., *South Africa: The Prospects of Peaceful Change* (London: Rex Collings, 1981); Professor L. Schlemmer, 'The report on the attitude surveys', Chapter 3 in *The Buthelezi Commission*, Vol. I (Durban: H + H Publications, ?1982).

3 Schlemmer, 'The report on the attitude surveys', *op. cit.*, p.243.

4 'Inkatha condemns ANC's "death call"', *The Citizen*, 16 September 1985; 'Power, liberation and the soft underbelly', *Business Day*, 3 September 1985; 'Buthelezi warns of "black civil war"', *The Star*, 23 July 1985; 'ANC and NP the "true victims of apartheid"', *The Star*, 15 January 1986. For a UDF view of Inkatha, see 'Government can't ban UDF spirit', *The Star*, 29 August 1985. For the ANC view of Buthelezi, see Patrick Laurence, 'Tambo speech scuttles hopes for Inkatha peace', *Weekly Mail*, 17-23 January 1986.

5 *Race Relations Survey 1984* (Johannesburg: SA Institute of Race Relations, 1985), pp.913-914; 'Chief hits at Tutu for backing ANC', *The Star*, 24 January 1986.

6 Hanf et al., *op. cit.*, p.340.

7 *Ibid.*, pp.243-244.

8 Schlemmer, 'The report on the attitude surveys', *op. cit.*, p.244.

9 *Ibid.*

10 'Tutu hits at critics after controversial fundraising tour', *The Star*, 10 February 1986.

11 *Ibid.*; Carol Lazar, 'A day in the life of Tutu', *The Sunday Star*, 10 November 1985.

12 Hannes de Wet, 'Flaws in arguments linking ANC and UDF pointed out', *The Star*, 25 September 1985; Sue Leeman, 'Ex-spy says UDF not wing of ANC', *The Star*, 9 January 1986. For a UDF statement on the alleged linkage, see John MacLennan, 'Brown Pimpernel drops out of the blue to push the UDF', *The Sunday Star*, 8 December 1985.

13 'Divide and revolt', *Financial Mail*, 3 May 1985; Jon Qwelane, 'Blacks from all over SA listen when Baba speaks', *The Sunday Star*, 26 January 1986.

14 'Bombs, bombast and the ANC's path', *The Star*, 12 January 1986.

15 *Survey of Race Relations in South Africa 1983* (Johannesburg: SA Institute of Race Relations, 1984), pp.316-318.

16 *Race Relations Survey 1984* (Johannesburg: SA Institute of Race Relations, 1985), p.528. For recent statements see 'Inkatha is still striving for change without violence', *The Star*, 17 August 1985, and 'Interview: Mangosuthu Buthelezi', *Leadership*, 4:4 (1985), 22-29 (p.26).

17 Harry Oppenheimer, 'Disinvestment - will it conduce to peace and justice in South Africa?', *Leadership* (June 1985), 8-14 (p.13).

18 Peter Honey, 'Urban Foundation's agenda for reform', *Business Day*, 21 August 1985.

19 Alan Paton, *Federation or Desolation* (Johannesburg: SA Institute of Race Relations, 1985), p.7. John Kane-Berman, Director of the SA Institute of Race Relations, takes a similar view in 'The crumbling of apartheid', *Leadership*, 4:4 (1985), 55-59 (p.59).

20 Patrick Laurence, 'The three hidden pledges in PW's speech', *Weekly Mail*, 4-10 October 1985.

21 Schlemmer, 'The report on the attitude surveys', *op. cit.*, p.261.

22 See, for example, *Survey of Race Relations in South Africa 1983* (Johannesburg: SA Institute of Race Relations, 1984), p.346; *Race Relations Survey 1984* (Johannesburg: SA Institute of Race Relations), p.529. For more recent statements, see Mangosuthu G. Buthelezi, 'Inkatha says no', *Leadership* (June 1985), 66-68 (p.66) and 'It's now the democratic process versus violence', *The Star*, 30 January 1986. A very explicit declaration has been made by Dr Oscar Dhlomo, 'The case for Inkatha', *The Star*, 24 February 1986.

Chapter 4

Conclusion: The Mainstream versus The System

We have now seen how urban blacks' political affiliations correlate with their views on the means and ends of social change, i.e. with the strategies being employed and the outcomes being sought. These patterns will now let us make sense of some recent political developments, link them to our initial concern with disinvestment, and thereby identify a fundamentally new configuration of conflict emerging in the South African context which has profound policy implications.

Prompted by mounting pressures for disinvestment the private sector in South Africa acquired a sudden new zest for change. During the South African visit of Senator Edward Kennedy early in 1985, the three major business federations — English-speaking, Afrikaans-speaking and African — achieved unprecedented accord in attacking his enthusiasm for economic sanctions, while at the same time calling on the government to accelerate its reform programme.[1] Important business delegations travelling abroad subsequently adopted a similar approach.[2] Then Judge Jan Steyn, Executive Chairman of the Urban Foundation, conceded at mid-year (at which juncture several hundred people had already died in the unrest since the elections for the tricameral parliament) that business, in supporting the new constitutional dispensation, had seriously underestimated black opposition to it.[3] With the imposition of the State of Emergency, the three business federations again united in a call for rapid reform.[4] After the collapse of the rand and the onset of the loans crisis, these appeals became quite frantic.[5]

During this period Chief Buthelezi had undertaken a flurry of trips abroad to lobby against disinvestment, greatly endearing him to business. At mid-year he indicated that because the new constitutional dispensation was by then on the statute book, he would be prepared to go along with it, despite his previously strenuous opposition, provided that it was extended and enlarged to allow for genuine power-sharing with Africans.[6]

These parallel developments coalesced in September 1985 in the Convention Alliance. Important business figures, the Progressive Federal Party, and leading English-speaking and 'verligte' Afrikaans-speaking academics and professionals endeavoured to meet 'moderate' black leaders towards arranging a national convention, in which agreement would be sought on non-violent means to end apartheid. However, the UDF declared that the proposal was an insult to its many leaders who were in detention or exile and so could not consider whether to participate.[7] Bishop Tutu was reported to have sent his blessings, but was conspicuous by his absence. The ANC announced that it was only interested in a national convention at which power would be handed over to the majority representatives of the people.[8] The only black leader of any note who was prepared to participate in the Alliance was Buthelezi.

The contrast between his response and that of the mainstream tendencies becomes intelligible in the light of the evidence we have laid out. His adherents overwhelmingly agree with his declared opposition to armed struggle and violence against the system. They favour strikes and sanctions much less than the mainstream. And they support the enthusiasm for federalism which he shares with the organized business community. The problem for the Alliance — and for any similar business, PFP, or 'verligte' initiative in future — is that although the proportion of urban blacks who support this sort of policy package may be somewhat larger than the 8% nationwide who support Buthelezi and Inkatha, and even as much as the 20% who support federalism, it is decidedly still a minority. And the representatives of the majority will not participate as long as Buthelezi is involved.

Having learned this lesson, the PFP and Inkatha representatives left the Alliance management committee in the hope that the radical groupings would join the movement. But the latter did not relent. The example usefully illustrates the relevance of our data: in its intention, the Alliance revealed the guiding interests of the minority parties which were ready to participate; and by its failure it confirmed the coherence, strength and popular legitimacy of the mainstream majority which refused.

It follows that if a broad-based alliance is to succeed, it will have to include the ANC and the other mainstream tendencies, and we have just seen that it will therefore exclude Buthelezi and Inkatha.[9] It was perhaps with some awareness of this implication that leading business figures began to cover their future options, and trekked to Lusaka to meet with Oliver Tambo and his senior colleagues on the ANC executive. The meeting was apparently convivial, and the two sides agreed on the importance of the government's releasing Mandela.[10] But the ANC was adamant that its recourse to violence was justifiable in the South African circumstances, and it reaffirmed its policy, albeit in euphemistic terms, that it would not allow ownership of the mines and farms to remain as narrowly concentrated as at present.[11] Subsequently, Gavin Relly of Anglo American dismissed this commitment as an obsolete dalliance with communism,[12] and some of the businessmen who went to the meeting have been reported as regretting their overture[13] following the ANC's renewed commitment to 'people's war' early in 1986.[14]

However, there were then rumours that the Convention Alliance was seeking links with the ANC,[15] and Advocate Jules Browde, the chief organizer, followed the path to Lusaka.[16] An alternative speculation was that a different popular front was to be constituted, involving the ANC and the organizations that had refused to join the Convention Alliance, and perhaps the PFP ... but not Inkatha.[17] However, the ANC itself dismissed the rumours as 'premature'.[18]

In the meanwhile, Buthelezi was not inactive. At a national level his response to the growing acknowledgement of the importance of the ANC seemed to be to try and drive a wedge, at least in the minds of his followers, between Nelson Mandela and the ANC leaders in Lusaka. On the one hand, he included the release of Mandela as a further precondition of his entering negotiations about power-sharing, and publicized a fraternal exchange of letters between himself and Mandela while the latter was receiving medical treatment in hospital.[19] Inkatha went so far as to commission a plaque commemorating the event.[20]

On the other hand, Buthelezi began pointedly to refer to the Lusaka contingent as the 'ANC mission in exile', and confirmed the hostility between himself and them by alleging that they were 'actually committed to annihilating Inkatha'.[21] And he subsequently condemned Bishop Tutu's call for Western governments to side with the ANC as 'divisive and a prescription for violence'.[22]

On the trade union front, Buthelezi attacked COSATU, the new umbrella trade union federation launched in December 1985, for its criticism of homeland leaders, its links to the UDF, and its advocacy of forms of disinvestment, and accused it of being a front for the ANC.[23] At the same time, it was announced that a new Inkatha-sponsored union, the United Workers' Union of South Africa (UWUSA), would be officially launched by Chief Buthelezi on 1st May. A prominent Inkatha businessman who regards strikes as 'irresponsible'[24] is at the head of UWUSA. He conceives the new union, in its fight against disinvestment and socialism, as being firmly opposed to COSATU.[25] This development exemplifies, to the point of caricature, the fact we noted at Figure 8 in Chapter 3, that by comparison with the mainstream Buthelezi's supporters tend to provide a conciliatory and strike-free workforce.

At the same time that Buthelezi was emphasizing his enmities, he began to cement his alliances, in his attempts to give effect to his federalist vision at a regional level. Months of meetings between the KwaZulu and Natal administrations resulted in an agreement to establish a Joint Executive Authority for the region.[26] The plan was that there would be equal representation for KwaZulu and Natal on the Authority; that decisions would be by 'consensus'; and that deadlocks would be referred to the Administrator of Natal and the Chief Minister of KwaZulu for joint decisions.[27] The proposal was presented to the government in March 1986.

As the most ardent proponents of the plan conceded, its central failing was that it would give power to the two existing administrations, and ultimately to two individuals, 'without the democratic process of elections'.[28] So a further phase was initiated. Beginning in April, an 'indaba', i.e. a series of meetings, was scheduled, to try and reach agreement about the form of a single legislature for the region.[29] Organized commerce and industry, from the Afrikaanse Handelsinstituut to the Zulu Cane-growers' Association, accepted their invitations. Not surprisingly, the indaba received an enormous fanfare in the business controlled English-speaking press.[30]

It was reported that all political groupings active in the region were also invited. However, the ANC, the UDF and AZAPO dismissed the entire proceeding. In their view it was 'divisive'.[31] The same view is quite widely held in KwaZulu: as we noted in passing at the end of the previous section, Buthelezi's own Commission found that only about a quarter of KwaZulu residents, whether rural or urban, declared themselves happy with precisely the sort of plan he is seeking to implement.

These developments on the political, labour, and constitutional fronts therefore have explosive implications for Natal. Buthelezi's invitation of some mainstream movements to the indaba may have been a disingenuous stratagem, in order to make short-term capital out of their inevitable refusal. But their non-participation will have very real long-term consequences. For, as we showed in Figures 5 and 6, the mainstream tendencies now outnumber Buthelezi's support in the urban townships of the region. In their absence, the proposed legislative assembly will aggravate the problem it is allegedly intended to solve, of providing 'fundamental legitimacy in an elected body for the whole region'.[32] The region will thus ultimately be ruled by coercion rather than consent. Far from being 'a chance for sanity',[33] this is a recipe for violence in the streets[34] and − with the likelihood of 'direct confrontation'[35] between COSATU and UWUSA, if the latter finds enough members − on the shop-floor.

In general it becomes evident that, although Buthelezi indubitably remains opposed to the government's original conception of homeland independence, in his current manoeuvres he is throwing in his lot with what the black students call 'the system', and what C. Wright Mills identified as the shared interest in capitalism among the agencies of economic, military and political power.[36] On the other hand, the ANC retains a commitment to socialism, which is shared not only by the non-racial UDF in its admiration for the Freedom Charter, but also by the other pro-disinvestment radical groups and unions, and by Bishop Tutu, who has lately affirmed his broad belief in socialism on account of its egalitarian and humanitarian thrust.[37]

Now it has always been the case that wrapped inside the overt racial conflict about political power between black and white in South Africa has been a conflict over material resources, initially between colonizer and colonized on the land and subsequently also between capital and labour in the mines and the factories.[38] It would now appear that the racial husk is splitting open, and that the participants themselves increasingly perceive that the struggle for political power coincides with the struggle for economic control: the system, comprising government and business and their allies such as Buthelezi who avowedly favour free enterprise,[39] versus the mainstream black political tendencies which seek to curtail the excesses of capitalism or replace it by a socialist alternative.

It is in pursuit not only of democratic political rights but also of these more or less explicitly socialist aims that most of the black political mainstream — followers of the ANC, of Bishop Tutu, and of the UDF and other radical groups — support conditional or total disinvestment amongst other strategies for social change. These are the imperatives which policy-makers must respect if they wish to accord with the clear majority opinion of blacks in metropolitan South Africa, and thereby help avert what Beyers Naudé, General Secretary of the SACC, has identified as an incipient civil war.[40]

Notes

1 Assocom, the Afrikaanse Handelsinstituut and the National African Chambers of Commerce were joined in this move by the Federated Chambers of Industries, the Chamber of Mines and the Steel and Engineering Industries. See 'Kennedy: employers get a word in' and 'Kennedy is pre-empted on reform call', *The Star*, 8 January 1985.

2 'SA businessmen speak against sanctions at UN', *The Star*, 19 September 1985; 'Delegation warns UK against punitive actions', *The Star*, 25 September 1985; 'Political signals suggested', *The Star*, 26 September 1985.

3 Reaction to new Parliament "badly underestimated"', *The Star*, 3 September 1985.

4 'Negotiate now, say businessmen', *The Star*, 30 August 1985; Melanie Gosling, 'Simple reason behind it all: the heat's on business', *The Sunday Star*, 22 December 1985.

5 Jenni Tennant, 'Ackerman urges Govt: now's the time to take action', *The Star*, 21 September 1985.

6 Peter Wallington, 'Buthelezi's action plan', *Business Day*, 25 July 1985.

7 'Convention: UDF warns PFP, Inkatha', *Cape Times*, 5 September 1985.

8 'Apartheid must go first', *The Sunday Star*, 29 September 1985.

9 Caroline Hurry, 'Buthelezi says yes again while UDF rejects Alliance', *The Sunday Star*, 29 September 1985.

10 'Business to push for Mandela's release', *The Star*, 16 September 1985.

11 'Businessmen hopeful after meeting ANC', *The Star*, 14 September 1985; 'The ANC spells it out to the bosses', *City Press*, 15 September 1985.

12 David Braun, 'We need a free market and a free society', *The Sunday Star*, 8 December 1985. See also 'Anglo chief defends ANC talks', *The Citizen*, 16 September 1985.

13 'Talks with ANC now regretted by businessmen', *The Citizen*, 17 January 1986.

14 'ANC to intensify "liberation struggle"', *The Star*, 9 January 1986; 'Tambo predicts more Toti-type bomb attacks', *The Star*, 10 January 1986.

15 'ANC, Convention movement want alliance talks', *The Sunday Star*, 19 January 1986.

16 'Tambo and Browde at Lusaka meeting', *The Sunday Star*, 26 January 1986.

17 'ANC "grand alliance" bid', *Sunday Times*, 12 January 1986.

18 'No chance of ANC "grand alliance" at this stage', *The Sunday Star*, 12 January 1986.

19 Max du Preez, 'ANC-Inkatha "pen pals" poser', *Sunday Times*, 19 January 1986.

20 'Inkatha to mark Mandela "bond"', *The Star*, 13 January 1986.

21 'Violence not the answer to SA problems – Buthelezi', *The Star*, 24 December 1985.

22 Mike Siluma, 'Chief hits at Tutu for backing ANC', *The Star*, 24 January 1986.

23 Sheryl Raine, 'New trade union formed in Natal', *The Star*, 24 February 1986.

24 Mike Siluma, 'Capitalist now unionist', *The Star*, 5 April 1986.

25 'New union will oppose socialism', *The Star*, 18 March 1986; 'New union may spell trouble', *The Star*, 19 March 1986.

26 David Breier, 'Inkatha bidding for its slice of Natal banana', *The Sunday Star*, 16 March 1986; Daryl Glaser, 'KwaNatal: the footsie-footsie option', *Weekly Mail*, 4-10 April 1986.

27 Jean Le May, 'Nats dead-keen to talk away Natal', *Weekly Mail*, 14-20 March 1986.

28 Lawrence Schlemmer, 'Indaba of hope', *Sunday Times*, 30 March 1986.

29 'Buthelezi gives Govt ultimatum on kwaNatal talks', *The Star*, 10 March 1986.

30 Schlemmer, 'Indaba of hope', *op. cit.*; Chief Mangosuthu Buthelezi, 'A chance for sanity', *The Sunday Star*, 30 March 1986.

31 Buthelezi, 'A chance for sanity', *op. cit.*

32 Schlemmer, 'Indaba of hope', *op. cit.*

33 Buthelezi, 'A chance for sanity', *op. cit.*

34 How events might unfold was perhaps adumbrated in April 1986, when three bus-loads of men set upon delegates at a conference in Durban of the UDF-affiliated National Education Crisis Committee (NECC). Buthelezi denied that he or Inkatha's central committee had organized the attack. Police spokesmen identified the attackers (two of whom died in the clash) as being Inkatha members, and the bus company confirmed that the vehicles had been hired by Inkatha. Buthelezi retorted that 'If there were Inkatha youths with Inkatha uniforms involved in the eruption of anger, why must I be blamed for their behaviour? The NECC itself came here [to Natal] to court anger.' See Patrick Laurence, 'Back to school for spirit of defiance', *Weekly Mail*, 4-10 April 1986.

35 Michael Chester, 'Management must talk to unions – expert', *The Star*, 13 March 1986.
36 C. Wright Mills, *The Power Elite* (New York: Oxford University Press, 1956).
37 Estelle Trengove, 'Tutu envisages a system of socialism in South Africa', *The Star*, 3 September 1985.
38 See, for example, F.A. Johnstone, 'Class conflict and colour bars in the South African gold mining industry 1910-1926' (Institute of Commonwealth Studies seminar paper, 1970); John Rex, 'The plural society: the South African case', in Adrian Leftwich (ed.), *South Africa: Economic Growth and Political Change* (London: Allison and Busby, 1974); H. Wolpe, 'The theory of colonialism: the South African case', in I. Oxaal et al. (eds), *Beyond the Sociology of Development* (London: Routledge, 1975); S. Greenberg, *Race and State in Capitalist Development* (Yale University Press, 1980).
39 See, for example, Mangosuthu G. Buthelezi, 'Inkatha says no', *Leadership* (June 1985), 66-68 (p.66); Dr Oscar Dhlomo, 'The case for Inkatha', *The Star*, 24 February 1986.
40 Nat Diseko, 'Hit SA harder – SACC', *The Star*, 30 June 1985; Beyers Naudé, 'Statements to the delegation of the EEC regarding the current crisis in South Africa', mimeo, 30 August 1985. For a similar characterization, see Tom Lodge, '"Soft" targets', *The South Africa Foundation News*, August 1985.

Appendix

Abbreviations

AFM	Apostolic Faith Mission
ANC	African National Congress
AZAPO	Azanian People's Organization
AZASM	Azanian Students Movement
AZASO	Azanian Students Organization
BC	Black Consciousness
CASE	Community Agency for Social Enquiry
COSAS	Congress of South African Students
COSATU	Congress of South African Trade Unions
CUSA	Council of Unions of South Africa
EEC	European Economic Community
FOSATU	Federation of South African Trade Unions
GM	General Motors
HSRC	Human Sciences Research Council
IBR	Institute for Black Research
ILO	International Labour Organization
NECC	National Education Crisis Committee
NP	National Party
OFS	Orange Free State
PAC	Pan African Congress
PFP	Progressive Federal Party
PWV	Pretoria-Witwatersrand-Vaal
SA	South Africa
SABC	South African Broadcasting Corporation
SACC	South African Council of Churches
UDF	United Democratic Front
UDI	Unilateral Declaration of Independence
UN	United Nations
US	United States

Methodological note

The questionnaire for this study was designed by the author of this report, the director of CASE, with the assistance of researchers of the IBR, trade unionists, representatives of community organizations, and experts on black political movements. The English phrasing and the translations into Sotho and Zulu were vetted by native speakers with a training in English second-language teaching. The main questions are listed in the last section of this Appendix.

Research Surveys (Pty) Limited, the largest independent South African market research agency, devised the sampling, conducted the nation-wide interviews, and executed the coding and computation, all in detailed consultation with the author.

The sample comprised 800 black respondents over sixteen years of age, including workers, unemployed, women, students, and pensioners. Respondents were selected by random area sample, proportionately stratified across all ten major metropolitan areas. These areas included 12,9 million blacks in 1984. The advantage of stratification is that it yields more accuracy than simple random sampling for the same number of cases.[1]

For the analysis, the areas were combined into three coherent regions. The PWV region comprised Pretoria, Johannesburg and Soweto, the Reef and the Vaal triangle; the Natal region, Durban and Pietermaritzburg; and the Cape region, Cape Town, Port Elizabeth and East London. Respondents from the tenth area, Bloemfontein, formed too small a proportion to be analysed separately, and were included with the PWV. The breakdown of respondents by region is shown in Table 8 in the next section of this Appendix, together with other sample characteristics.

The sample size ensures that, 95% of the time, the percentage margin of error on any particular response is at most 4%, and usually better than 3%.

The field-work was conducted early in September 1985. Respondents were interviewed face-to-face. Their subsequent anonymity was assured, after the supervisors had conducted spot checks on a tenth of the interviews, by our removing and destroying the special top sheet of the questionnaire, which contained respondents' names and addresses. Interviews were conducted in the evenings (before the curfew hour which was imposed during the State of Emergency!) and at the week-end, to try to avoid skewing the sample away from prospective respondents who would be at work or school during week-days.

The interviewers reported that substitutions had to be sought for less than one in five of sampled respondents, much the same refusal rate as is customarily encountered in uncontentious product surveys. What was different from the interviewers' usual commercial experience was that respondents tended to be very earnest about considering the questions, and insistent that their replies be transcribed in detail. The interviews lasted for three-quarters of an hour, on average. It was clear that, for blacks whose opinions are systematically ignored by the authorities, the opportunity to express considered views on important issues was in most instances regarded as a worthwhile and affirmative occasion.

It is quite possible, as commentators abroad tend to emphasize,[2] that state terror in South Africa might intimidate some respondents towards conservative replies. In a less repressive context, the patterns of replies might well have been even bolder than those sketched in this report. But it seems more likely, as Schlemmer has remarked,[3] that respondents will rather fend off any question they consider intrusive or risky with the answer 'I don't know'.

There are two empirical indications that any conservative bias in this study is actually slight. Firstly, the proportion of 'no answers' is only a few per cent for all but the most controversial question, on respondents' personal leadership affiliation. (The disinvestment question turned out not to be threatening in the eyes of respondents. Although high-profile spokesmen understandably make much of the possible penalties for publicly advocating disinvestment,[4] the 1% no-answer rate to this question shows that individual respondents had little hesitation about expressing a private opinion.)[5]

Secondly, when one examines how the respondents who declined to answer the leadership question answered other key questions, e.g., on disinvestment or the justifiability of armed struggle, one finds that the distribution of their opinions is very similar to that of the overall sample. Since leadership choice is highly associated with these other key issues, one may infer that the fraction of 'no answers' is not appreciably higher among the politically more vulnerable tendencies.

However, there is a different potential bias in our data: the apparently rather high proportion of CASE/IBR respondents with matric or better, as shown in Table 8 in the next section. This probably arose as follows. Our area sampling involved a random choice of squares on regional map grids, then of dwellings on random walks within the indicated squares, and finally of individuals within the dwellings. Until the necessary information is publicly available for one to correct for the density of housing and of occupancy across townships nation-wide, such area sampling will have the consequence that individuals who can afford to live in comparatively small households on comparatively large plots of land — i.e. people whose better education has won them more income — will tend to come up in the sample more often than is their random due.

One could have sought to guard against this skew by quota-sampling, or else have corrected for it *ex post facto* by appropriately weighting the data. However, statistical testing for significance, to establish whether one may generalize from one's sample to the population, is invalidated by either stratagem.[6] Moreover, one has to use the census as the base-line for the quotas or the corrections. In South Africa this is, as we shall note below, rather like the blind leading the lame. Ignoring the educational imbalance would therefore be preferable, provided it did not seriously affect our findings.

We must therefore test the proviso: how, and by how much, might the results be biassed by this feature of our sample? The argument on these questions is rather technical. But, to put the conclusion bluntly, it will show that if our sampling is off course, given the field information available to us, (a) we are not much further off course than others who might claim to be on; and (b) for our purposes it makes a negligible difference anyway.

We begin by considering the *direction* of the possible bias. For the case of urban black South Africans, the HSRC suggests that the more educated the respondents, the more radically opposed to the status quo they will be.[7] This is largely borne out by our data, for example on the disinvestment issue, as Table 6 indicates.

Table 6 Attitudes to disinvestment, by education[a]

Favoured option	Up to Std 6 %	Form I-IV %	Form V+ %
Free investment	33	25	18
Conditional disinvestment	48	48	57
Total disinvestment	19	26	25
	100	99	100
	(n=196)	(n=330)	(n=274)

[a]Chi-squared = 24 for 4 d.f., p = .0001

Reading across the first row of the table, one sees that the proportion in favour of the conservative option, free investment, decreases from a third through a quarter to less than a fifth with increasing education. Conversely, the proportions in favour of conditional and total disinvestment both increase, albeit less smoothly, with increasing education. Thus, if the less-educated were under-represented in our sample, the disinvestment options would in fact receive less support in the urban population than our sample suggests.

We can now consider to what *extent* this educationally-based radical bias may affect our final results. To be sure of this, we would need to know the actual distribution of educational qualifications among urban blacks. The 1980 census provides a publicly available official answer, but not necessarily a definitive one. Its most serious deficiency was under-enumeration, to the extent that it was felt necessary to repeat the entire exercise subsequently.

Although the census reports claim to correct for this, there remains the problem that the missing counts may not have been evenly distributed across the categories at issue. For instance, the considerable proportion of people living in the townships 'illegally', in contravention of the influx control laws, are understandably reluctant to be counted by government officials. What the hidden loading might be in respect of education is more difficult to foresee.

So let us contemplate the census data in the light of three major sample surveys. The survey evidence confines our comparison to urban black adults in the PWV. Table 7 sets out the distributions of education obtained by the

Table 7 Distribution of urban blacks' education in the PWV: comparison of three studies with the census

Educational level	Census[a] 1980 %	Schlemmer[b] 1981 %	HSRC[c] 1984-5 %	CASE/IBR[d] 1985 %
Up to Std 6	65	41	54	30
Form I to Form IV	32	39	34	40
Form V +	3	20	12	30
	100	100	100	100
		(n=612)	(n=2577)	(n=563)

[a] Five per cent sample of the enumeration; 20 years and older. (For comparison with the surveys, we need a break-down by age, to extract the figures for adults only. The published tables do not provide this age break-down for the various areas making up the PWV. But they do provide it for the nation-wide urban figures. The latter are thus quoted in the table above. They are, however, likely to be a good approximation of education among urban adults in the PWV, because the available tables do show that the education distributions for all ages barely differ between the PWV and the nation-wide instances.)

[b] Quota sample, unspecified control variables; 18 years and older.

[c] Mean of two random samples proportionately stratified by area, and using addresses of dwellings within census districts; 18 years and older.

[d] Random sample proportionately stratified by area, and using random walks within map grid squares; 16 years and older.

census[8] in 1980, Schlemmer's study for the Buthelezi Commission[9] in 1981, two of the HSRC's disinvestment surveys[10] in 1984-5, and the relevant subset of the CASE/IBR study in 1985.

Since the percentages in the intermediate educational category of the table do not vary widely, we may conveniently summarize the differences among the four distributions by the ratio of the least-educated to the best-educated. This is more than 20:1 for the census, compared to 2:1, 5:1 and 1:1 for the Schlemmer, HSRC and CASE/IBR studies. In this respect the studies clearly differ much less from each other than they do from the census. (The HSRC samples are least distant from the official figures, no doubt because the HSRC used census districts and addresses, to which it had access.) It would of course be rash to conclude from this evidence alone that the census is wrong. However, it does not provide an indisputable baseline either, because of the unknown pattern of under-enumeration.

So rather than argue the merits of one source or another, let us take the worst available instance and calculate the possible effect of the disparities on a couple of our key results. The biggest differences are between the CASE/IBR and the census distributions.

Given the percentage preferences of CASE/IBR respondents across the disinvestment options for each educational stratum, set out in Table 6, the arithmetic shows that if the census's educational proportions for urban black adults, as listed in Table 7, had prevailed in our sample, the outcome would have been 33%, 46% and 21% for free investment, conditional disinvestment, and total disinvestment respectively. These scores are not far from our own of 26%, 49% and 24%, reported in Chapter 2. In other words, even if the composite fraction in favour of some or other form of disinvestment is not as much as three-quarters, it is at least two-thirds. (Had Schlemmer's education proportions prevailed, the outcome would have been 29%, 48% and 23%. In this case, the discrepancies become less than our probable sampling margins of error.)

Corresponding calculations for the leadership question also show the variations to be trivial. When one applies the census educational distribution to our data, it yields 28% support for Mandela and the ANC (compared to 31% in the CASE/IBR study), 16% for Bishop Tutu (16%), 9% for the UDF and radical groups (14%), and 9% for Chief Buthelezi and Inkatha (8%). The remaining categorizations, mainly no answers, total 38% (32% for CASE/IBR).

It is just as we would have expected from Table 6: a sample more inclined to the less-educated slightly boosts the more conservative (or more hesitant) options. What is most noteworthy is how minor the effect turns out to be.

Surely the effect should have been greater, since the differences in the samples in respect of education seem to be considerable, and education is significantly associated with the attitudes concerned? The question manifests a common confusion. There is a world of difference between the *significance* of an association (which is what signals that one may generalize the finding from the particular sample to the wider population) and the *strength* of the association. Significance is related to sample size, so that with the large samples used in a nation-wide survey, even weak effects may be significant in the precise statistical sense defined above. But weak effects are usually unimportant for one's substantive considerations. Conversely, as we have now seen in respect of education, unless the 'pull' of a variable is strong as well as significant, its actual effect on the variable which one is measuring will not be appreciable.[11]

This pragmatic orientation would be inadequate in attempting to predict a US Presidential election, in which a swing of a couple of points can make all the difference. But it is, we maintain, both necessary and appropriate in the context of making independent quantitative macro-sociology available to those who need it in a third-world police-state. The relative percentage scores we obtained have turned out to be impressively robust across the sort of sampling differences that crop up in practice, and quite adequate for identifying broad majorities favouring or opposing particular proposals. Of course it is desirable to be as precise as possible about the technicalities of selecting people to question. But the above calculations confirm that sensible results depend to a much greater extent, as we showed in Chapter 2, on plausible intuitions for matching the form of the questions to one's respondents' historically developing frame of reference.[12]

Notes

1 Hubert M. Blalock Jr, *Social Statistics* (Kogakusha: McGraw-Hill, 1979), p.560. Because of the anxieties about the census discussed in this section, the population distribution reflected in Table 8 was derived from the *AMPS (All Media Products Survey) Technical Report* (Sandton: SA Advertising Research Foundation Ltd, 1984), Table 62D/4.

2 New York Correspondent, 'Disinvestment and black workers: a critique of the Schlemmer report', *South African Labour Bulletin*, 10:6 (May 1985), 43-53 (p.49). See also Sam Nolutshungu, quoted in M.O. Sutcliffe and P.A. Wellings, 'Disinvestment and black worker "attitudes" in South Africa: a critical comment', forthcoming in *Review of African Political Economy*.

3 Lawrence Schlemmer, Document and Memorandum Series of the Centre for Applied Social Science at the University of Natal, July 1985, p.5.

4 David Braun, 'Encouraging disinvestment a crime?', *The Star*, 14 December 1984; Estelle Trengove, 'Will Tutu's call for sanctions put him in danger of a prosecution?', *The Star*, 3 April 1986.

5 Compare Schlemmer, *op. cit.*, p.6.

6 Blalock, *op. cit.*, p.571. Schlemmer seems to be confused on this point. In one piece, 'The report on the attitude surveys', Chapter 3 in *The Buthelezi Commission*, Vol. I (Durban: H + H Publications, ?1982), he mentions using a quota sample (p.194), and then promises that generalizations will only be offered if based on differences calculated to be statistically significant (p.196). However, in his paper 'Disinvestment and black worker attitudes in South Africa: rejoinder to critical comment by M.O. Sutcliffe and P.A. Wellings', *op. cit.*, he correctly notes apropos his first disinvestment study that 'it is not appropriate to perform statistical tests on quota samples, hence I did not do so' (p.3).

7 Chris de Kock et al., 'Volwasse Swartes in die Pretoria-Witwatersrand-Vaaldriehoekgebied se persepsies van ekonomiese boikotte teen Suid-Afrika: 'n vergelyking van drie opnames se gegewens', Human Sciences Research Council, Pretoria, mimeo, August 1985, pp.19-21.

8 Republic of South Africa, *Population Census 1980, Sample Tabulation: Social Characteristics*, Report No. 02-80-02 (Pretoria: Government Printer, n.d.), Table 11.

9 Professor L. Schlemmer, 'The report on the attitude surveys', *op. cit.*, p.412.

10 Chris de Kock et al., *op. cit.*

11 Unfortunately there is no single handy index of the strength with which two categorical variables are related. 'Different measures of association focus their attention on different aspects of the relation', so we 'should not be worried by differences in the magnitudes of the various measures' (G.J.G. Upton, *The Analysis of Cross-Tabulated Data* (Chichester: Wiley, 1978), p.22 and p.38). This is why we chose simply to display the likely outer limits of the possible effects of the bias.

12 The model of emancipatory social enquiry invoked in this conclusion derives partly from Jurgen Habermas's critical theory, set out in *Knowledge and Human Interests* (London: Heinemann, 1972), and usefully explicated by Brian Fay, *Social Theory and Political Practice* (London: Allen and Unwin, 1975). But, in the conviction that adequately grounded quantitative work is an essential component of the project, it owes even more to Karl-Otto Apel's *Analytic Philosophy of Language and the Geisteswissenschaften* (Dordrecht: Reidel, 1967).

Sample characteristics

Table 8 Demographic profile of CASE/IBR respondents

Category		Number	Per cent
Total		800	100
Age	16-24	246	31
	25-34	304	38
	35-49	194	24
	50+	56	7
Education	Up to Std 2	40	5
	Std 3-6	156	19
	Form I-IV	330	41
	Form V	215	27
	Further education	59	7
Ethnic group	Sotho	172	22
	Swazi	26	3
	Tswana	96	12
	Xhosa	171	21
	Zulu	282	35
	Other	53	7
Monthly income	Up to R200	81	10
	R200-R499	258	32
	R500-R799	245	31
	R800+	216	27
Region	PWV		
	Pretoria	78	10
	Johannesburg	55	7
	Soweto	164	21
	Reef and Vaal	266	33
	Natal		
	Durban	96	12
	Pietermaritzburg	16	2
	Cape		
	Cape Town	21	3
	East London	32	4
	Port Elizabeth	56	7
	Orange Free State		
	Bloemfontein	16	2

Table 8 Demographic profile of CASE/IBR respondents (continued)

Category		Number	Per cent
Religious affiliation	Anglican	100	13
	Black Independent	137	17
	Catholic	116	15
	Dutch Reformed	57	7
	Methodist, Baptist, Presbyterian	195	24
	None	75	9
	Other	120	15
Sex	Male	401	50
	Female	399	50

The questionnaire: main items

Question 1

(a) How do you feel about life in South Africa now? Would you say you are...?
   - Happy
   - Angry
   - Not happy and not angry: in the middle
(b) Think of the present time in South Africa, and everything that is happening now. Is life for you...?
   - Improving
   - Staying the same
   - Getting worse

Question 2

What are your main problems or grievances about how things are in South Africa today? [Open-ended question]
   - Economic: unemployment, unequal or low wages, cost of living, sales tax
   - Political: apartheid, racial discrimination, pass laws, no vote
   - The Emergency: police killing and beating, unrest and riots, curfew, banning of organizations, inter-black violence
   - Education: inferior quality, detention of pupils and teachers
   - Welfare: housing shortage, high rents, poor amenities
   - Other

Question 3

Which one leader or organization would you most like to represent you, in solving these problems or grievances? [Open question]

Question 4

When the South African government refuses to end apartheid, groups of people adopt different ways or strategies of pressuring them. Do you think black people are right or wrong in using the following strategies to pressure the government to change?
   - Direct action by blacks inside South Africa, such as strikes, boycotts of white businesses and protests against high rents and unequal education.
   - Armed struggle against the government's security forces.
   - Foreign or overseas pressure on businessmen to demand changes from the government.
   - Public demand for genuine negotiations between the government and true leaders of the black people.
   - Attacks on blacks who work for the system, such as community councillors and homeland authorities.

Question 5
See Table 1 in Chapter 2.

Question 6
We have asked you about foreign investment. We noted that some groups want to limit foreign investment or stop it altogether. This is called disinvestment. These groups want disinvestment in order to pressure the government to end apartheid. Do you think that disinvestment will actually help in pressuring the government to end apartheid?

- Yes
- No
- Don't know

Question 7
There has been discussion about disinvestment and jobs — some people say that disinvestment may cause some blacks to lose their jobs, but the sacrifice is worthwhile in order to pressure the government to end apartheid. If few blacks lose their jobs, is the sacrifice worthwhile? If many blacks lose their jobs, is the sacrifice worthwhile?

- 'Hard-line': 'yes' to both questions
- Intermediate: 'yes' to one question, and 'no' or 'don't know' to the other
- Cautious: 'no' to both questions

Question 8
People and groups in South Africa are discussing how quickly the apartheid system can be brought to an end. There are two main views. Which view do you most support?

- The first view is that it is unrealistic to expect whites to change overnight. People who support this view therefore suggest starting with a federal arrangement in which Africans are partly governed by homeland leaders, but also have some representation in the central government. This view is held by some members of the Nationalist Party and the PFP, many businessmen, and Chief Buthelezi's Inkatha movement.
- The second view is that compromise is no longer possible. People who support this view therefore believe that the next step must be a unitary arrangement in which all blacks and whites together vote for their leaders, to participate without regard to race or group in one central government for South Africa. This view is held by AZAPO, the UDF, the PAC, and the ANC.

Question 9

Suppose South Africa had the government of your choice. There are two main patterns how it should organize people's work, and the ownership of factories and businesses. Which view do you most support?

- the capitalist pattern, in which businesses are owned and run by private businessmen, for their own profit.
- the socialist pattern, in which workers have a say in the running of businesses, and share in the ownership and profits.

Index

76   *Index*

72
FOSATU, 7, 8
France, 26
free enterprise, *see* capitalism vs socialism
Freedom Charter, 41, 48, 58
future, the, 3, 33, 54
economic, socialism vs capitalism, 52,
73
political, federal vs unitary
dispensation, 18, 49-52, 72

Gallup, 5
General Motors, 18, 22
Genscher, Foreign Minister Hans-Dieter,
26
Germany, West, 26, 28
government, South African, 1-3, 7, 8, 16,
18, 23, 24, 27, 33-39, 50, 54, 58, 65,
72
grievances, 34, 35, 71

Hanf, Dr Theo et al., survey, 37-39, 42
hardship, *see* suffering
Helena Rubenstein, 21
HSRC, surveys, 5, 10, 43, 63-65

IBM, 22
IBR, *see* CASE/IBR
IMF, 18
indaba, 57
Inkatha, 1, 8, 35-39, 41, 43-47, 50, 55,
56, 66, 72; *see also* Buthelezi
investment
ban, 22, 25
capital-intensive, 18
composition, changing, 20
economic growth, 1, 8
employment, 1, 18
foreign, 1, 8, 18-20, 27
UK, level of, 25
unconditional, 5-8, 11-13, 15, 45, 46,
52, 64, 66, 72
US, level of, 20, 25

Japan, 27

Kennedy, Senator Edward, 5, 54
Kinnock, Neil, 26
Krugerrands, 22

KwaZulu, 1, 43, 51, 57
KwaZulu-Natal, joint arrangements, 51,
57

labour, migrant, 20
leaders, homeland, 8, 9, 37, 39, 50, 51,
56, 72
Leadership, 3
leadership, *see* tendencies, political
leadership, question, 34, 35, 63, 66, 71
life, in South Africa, 34, 71
loans, 8, 18, 20, 22, 27
crisis, 23, 24, 26, 27, 54

mainstream, the, 47-51, 54, 55, 57, 58
Mandela, Nelson, 2, 35-41, 44-47, 55,
56, 66; *see also* ANC
Mandela, Winnie, 2
mediator, Swiss, 24
Mills, C. Wright, 58
Moberley, Sir Patrick, 26
Mobil, 22, 24
Motlana, Dr Ntatho, 37
movements, *see* tendencies, political

Natal region, 6, 39-41, 47, 51, 57, 62, 69
National Forum, 48
Naudé, Dr Beyers, 24, 58
negotiations, genuine, 33, 34, 46, 71
Netherlands, The, 26
New Zealand, 26
Nickel, Ambassador Herman, 3

Observer, The, 26
Oppenheimer, Harry, 8, 22, 27, 50
opposition, official, 1

PAC, 2, 8, 19, 35-37, 50, 72
PanAm, 21
patents, 20
Paton, Dr Alan, 50
Pepsi Cola, 21
PFP, 50, 54-56, 72
Phibro-Salomon, 21
pressure, economic, 1, 20, 21, 27, 33,
34, 46, 47, 71
protests, *see* strikes, boycotts and protests
PWV region, 5, 6, 37, 38, 40, 41, 43,
51, 62, 64, 65, 69